Educational leadership in Aotearoa New Zealand:

Issues of context and social justice

Educational leadership in Aotearoa New Zealand:
Issues of context and social justice

Edited by
Rachel McNae, Michele Morrison, and Ross Notman

NZCER PRESS

NZCER PRESS
New Zealand Council for Educational Research
PO Box 3237
Wellington
New Zealand
www.nzcer.org.nz

ISBN 978-0-947509-67-5

A catalogue record for this book is available from the National
Library of New Zealand.

Designed by Smartwork Creative, www.smartworkcreative.co.nz

Whakataukī

Ehara taku toa, I te toa takitahi engari he toa takatini

My strength comes not from myself alone
but from the strength of the group

Contents

Foreword

As co-directors of the International School Leadership Development Network (ISLDN), we have watched the network grow from a passionate group of individual researchers to a cohesive and collaborative team investigating social justice leadership and high-needs schools across the world. As we have grown, the researchers from New Zealand have taken a lead role in guiding our understandings of the importance of context and culture in school leader agency with marginalised children. This work has culminated with the research studies captured in this book; specifically, social justice leadership in high-needs school settings throughout New Zealand. What is most encouraging to us is that the two separate strands of the ISLDN project—social justice leadership and high-needs school leadership—intersect in this volume. The qualitative case studies, described herein, of 10 New Zealand school leaders clearly demonstrate that social justice advocacy is essential, especially in high-needs schools and communities where families and their children encounter social and economic disadvantages.

Readers will find a rich contextual and cultural mix of cases, including early childhood centres; primary, intermediate, and secondary schools; ethnically diverse schools and communities; high and low decile schools; and secular and faith-based institutions. Although the findings from a handful of studies cannot be generalised to other school and community contexts, we believe readers will recognise the social conditions and individuals portrayed in these cases and will gain deep appreciation for the personal and professional dispositions of the school leaders. These women and men are not portrayed as heroines or heroes, but as compassionate human beings with a clear understanding of their context, strong belief in children's capabilities, and deep insights about their personal beliefs and actions.

Each case is intended to stand alone, yet the editors identify three overarching themes capturing the essence of social justice leadership: complexity, agency, and action. They deftly provide illustrations from the cases highlighting the complex external and internal contexts leaders must negotiate; the deep sense of moral purpose shaping their worldviews; and their commitment to parental involvement, collaboration, reflective practice, and long-term thinking. What clearly comes through in the analysis is the leaders' tireless advocacy for children's growth and development and their constant battle to overcome deficit thinking mindsets, substandard teaching practices, and misguided beliefs about parental and community engagement.

When examining the actions and dispositions of highly-effective school leaders, we are left wondering how they came to possess these skills and attitudes. We considered this same perplexing question after reading this book: Can social justice leadership be developed and learned? Or is this commitment innate, based on life experiences or other intangible events? While this is not the major purpose of this book, the authors provide a series of cogent recommendations about preparation and policy aimed at nurturing social justice leadership. Our sense is that school leaders see their work as a calling, rather than as a job or a profession.

While each case study stands alone in its unique context, the reader is presented with a plethora of rich stories and glimpses into the worlds of New Zealand school leaders as they work for social justice for children in high-needs schools. This book leaves us much to ponder and to appreciate.

Pamela Angelle
University of Tennessee, USA

Bruce Barnett
University of Texas at San Antonio, USA

August 2017

Acknowledgements

We would like to acknowledge with gratitude the contributions of the following individuals and organisations.

In their respective roles as directors of the social justice and high-needs strands of the International School Leadership Development Network project, Pamela Angelle (USA) and Bruce Barnett (USA) kindly agreed to write the foreword to this book.

The University of Waikato was the major research sponsor of the New Zealand social justice strand of the project and its editorial processes, while the University of Otago Research Fund provided financial support for the high-needs section of the project.

The National Council of the New Zealand Educational Administration and Leadership Society gave strategic support for the book's publication, in accord with its aim to enhance cross-sector understandings of educational leadership in New Zealand.

Students at Te Wharau School designed and created the mosaic on the front cover, gifting this taonga (treasure) to their school upon completing their primary schooling in 2005. The poutama (steps) depicting earth, land, and sky symbolise their love of heritage, environment, and learning.

Finally, we would like to record our appreciation to the contributors who willingly engaged in data gathering and analyses, and have reported their findings through a rich collection of cases. As an editorial team, we sincerely thank the educational leaders for sharing their stories of context and social justice with a much wider national and international audience.

Rachel McNae, Michele Morrison, and Ross Notman (Editors)

Chapter 1 Introduction: Leading for social justice and high needs in education

Ross Notman, Michele Morrison, and Rachel McNae

As educational inequities become apparent in global policy shifts, there have been calls in the literature of educational leadership for a closer examination of approaches to address such inequities. These calls have centred on strategies such as how to improve schools in challenging circumstances (Gurr & Day, 2014), how to turn schools around from levels of low performance (Leithwood, Harris, & Strauss, 2010), and educational leadership approaches used in the pursuit of social justice (Shields, 2014).

In 2010 the International School Leadership Development Network (hereafter referred to as ISLDN) was launched as an inter-country research partnership between the American University Council for Educational Administration (UCEA) and the British Educational Leadership, Management and Administration Society (BELMAS). Its broad purpose is to examine the preparation and development of educational leaders, school leaders in particular. Two research strands of the ISLDN have emerged from an initial series of international case studies: (1) the preparation and development of leaders who advance the cause of social justice in their schools; and (2) preparing and developing leaders to work in high-needs schools. The Social Justice Leadership strand comprises 28 researchers who have conducted interviews with principals in 20 different countries. Sixteen members of the High-Needs Schools' strand have carried out 22 studies in eight countries (Barnett & Stevenson, 2014).

Conceptual frameworks

The two major strands above inform the conceptual and research basis for this book. First, the conceptual framework of social justice has been variously defined in the literature. McNae (2014, p. 95) cites Lee's (2007) definition as encapsulating many of the discourses considered essential by scholars when describing social justice:

> Social justice involves promoting access and equity to ensure full
> participation in the life of a society, particularly for those who have
> been systematically excluded on the basis of race/ethnicity, gender,
> age, physical or mental disability, education, sexual orientation, socio-
> economic status, or other characteristics of background or group
> membership. Social justice is based on a belief that all people have a
> right to equitable treatment, support for their human rights, and fair
> allocation of societal resources. (Lee, 2007, p. 1)

In terms of linking leadership to social justice, Ryan (2006) offers a generic overview of such a linkage that is both idiosyncratic to the leaders themselves and situationally bound:

> Leadership and social justice are not natural bedfellows; nor are
> leadership and inclusion. The extent to which leadership meshes with
> social justice or inclusion depends on the way in which leadership
> is conceived, that is, in the way that relationships are envisioned
> among members of institutions, in the roles that are prescribed for
> individuals and groups, and in the ends to which leadership activities
> are directed. (p. 7)

Fullan (2015), one of the major writers in the field of educational leadership, has commented on the global context of social justice and leading for successful educational outcomes. He cites eight factors of whole-system change of which the following three factors are germane to this discussion. First, he points to a moral imperative for all students to learn, where every child can access the curriculum and enjoy success in it. Second, there is a necessity to build leadership at all levels of the institution. For example, Fullan (2015) sees that greater progress is made on the equity agenda when principals are proactively 'lead learners'— where they become more knowledgeable about problems to be solved 'on the ground'. Third, there is the factor of cultivating district-wide involvement, as can be seen in New Zealand in redesigned clusters of schools affected by the Christchurch earthquake. Fullan (2015) concludes that achieving greater equity for school students requires a system-wide focus that consists of features such as setting clear goals for improvement and monitoring system-wide results that can be used as levers for intervention: "This does not rule out strong intervention (to replace a principal, for example) but the overall emphasis must be on moving the whole system" (p. 53). Underlying these sentiments is the notion of educational leaders who are both transformative and ethical, a point reinforced by Shields (2012) in her distinction between a socially just education and a social justice education. The latter, she believes, "prepares students for life in a pluralistic society in which we must recognise our interdependence and global connectedness" (Shields, 2014, p. 39).

The second concept of high-needs in schools and the different facets of 'need' have informed the development of the high-needs strand. A major factor in a high-needs educational environment is uniformly acknowledged to be one of social and economic disadvantage for families within the school community. Mulford et al. (2008) summarise this overarching factor of disadvantage:

> Schools serving low SES [socioeconomic status] families can find themselves in an 'iron circle' that begins with the family's impoverished economic conditions that may involve unemployment, cultural, racial and/or linguistic factors, immigration, high mobility, family break-ups, malnutrition and other health problems, substance abuse, and low expectations including performance at school. (p. 462)

The concept of high need is also intertwined with the concept of students 'at risk' in their learning. 'At-risk' factors identified here include students with limited learning opportunities; minimal learning assistance in the home; limited financial and technological resources; and "lifestyle risk factors such as inadequate housing, frequent exposure to violence and poor nutritional habits" (Weldon, 2012, p. 1). In contrast, Shields and Edwards (2004) have advanced a critical perspective from their Canadian research that many conceptions of 'at riskness' promote deficit thinking, or rely on pathologising the lived experiences of children, thereby perpetuating educational strategies that may marginalise many of these young people.

Unsurprisingly, there is widespread support in the literature for the primacy of the principal's role in influencing learning in high-needs schools (for example, Day, 2007; Klar & Brewer, 2013). Consequently, there are also calls in the literature for broader forms of leadership development to enable school leaders to have greater contextual awareness and support culturally relevant pedagogy to meet students' learning needs (Bishop, 2011; Sleeter, 2012).

A third framework draws on a concept of contextually responsive leadership, whereby school leaders are 'contextually literate' through their capacity to understand, and respond to, challenges presented to them by the environment in which they work. For example, internal contexts within which principals operate can include the following influence factors: school culture; teacher experience and competence; staff morale; financial resourcing; school size; and bureaucratic organisation (Hallinger, 2003).

New Zealand educational context

Despite the challenges of educational underachievement for some students in New Zealand, it should be acknowledged that a greater proportion of students still rank highly on international measures such as PISA reports—the Programme for International Student Assessment, conducted by the Organisation for Economic Co-operation and Development (OECD), to study 15-year-old students' scholastic performance in reading, mathematics, and science. Overall national examination results are showing improvement; a focus on priority learners is now targeting areas of need, and student stand-downs and suspensions continue to decrease.

However, there remains considerable work to be done in New Zealand, as evidenced in the educational literature (for example, Carpenter & Osborne, 2014; Gordon, 2003). Raising student achievement—particularly in literacy and numeracy, and for groups of underperforming students (largely Māori, Pasifika, and students in poor communities)—still remains a system priority in New Zealand. Success continues to sit alongside challenge as we progress our strategies and thinking about educational improvement. In this contrasting environment of success and challenge in promoting social justice leadership and high-needs school leadership, Fullan's (2015) comments about whole-system reform find a parallel with Wylie's (2013) call for a systemic re-connection between schools and policy makers. For example, she advocates that the New Zealand Ministry of Education and local principals might engage jointly in reviewing an area's or region's student achievement progress and planning, such as "ensuring that all schools serving low-income and rural communities can attract and retain the teachers they need" (p. 48). It appears that educational success in social justice for high-need environments is as much about creative and collaborative futures thinking on a broader scale as it is about problem solving at the local level.

The New Zealand research context

In this New Zealand research environment, the ISLDN project has conducted two qualitative studies that focused on the respective research strands. First, during the period 2013–14, Morrison, McNae, and Branson (2015) initiated research into the Social Justice strand and gathered data from 15 school principals in the central North Island. As a broad summary of how the principal sample viewed the concept of social justice, they alluded to "due process and the right to be heard, to evening out economic, social and cultural disparities in ways that build community, and to releasing human potential" (p. 9). It was of interest that the group of principals noted a lack of professional learning opportunities and that, for some principals, issues of social justice rarely featured in principals' meetings they attended. They believed it was not only a government responsibility to address social justice challenges in education, but also a responsibility for principals and the role of the school to raise the focus of our thinking and our action about the topic. As one principal noted, "We can't just reflect society, we have to move it. It's our job to change it" (Morrison et al., 2015, p. 14).

In the absence of national policy statements and common consensus as to what social justice means, it is not surprising that participant definitions were personal, atheoretical, and somewhat tentative. The concern for equity permeating conceptions of social justice appeared grounded in lived and vicarious experiences that variously attuned principals to injustice and compelled them to confront this. Examples included social engagement that exposed idealistic notions of cultural inclusion, political events that provoked student activism, immigration that brought cultural and academic dislocation, and colleagues who sensitised leaders to issues they were previously oblivious to. The omission of formal teacher education and leadership preparation programmes as catalysts suggests either that these did not feature issues of social justice, or that coverage was minimal or insufficiently memorable in impact.

Research findings revealed that principals worked in multiple ways and on multiple fronts to: simultaneously disrupt racist, hegemonic and exclusionary practices; distribute resources in more equitable ways; drive improvement in relationships, pedagogy, and student attainment; and develop community. The factors enabling and constraining this work varied according to context. Whereas committed and innovative staff sustained and accelerated change initiatives in some settings, leaders perceived teacher intransigence to be a major impediment in others. Whereas cohesion enabled concerted community and inter-agency responses in some settings, fractured relationships required mending in others. These are but two of many examples illustrating the situated and temporal nature of leading for social justice. They serve to highlight the crucial importance of accurately discerning context, determining immediate need, and prioritising goals accordingly.

The relentless pursuit of social justice outcomes required, in addition to strategic and managerial skills, a willingness to speak out, agitate, and advocate, both within the school and beyond. Such a commitment demanded of these school leaders considerable resolve, courage, resilience, and, on occasion, self-sacrifice. Leading for social justice was a daily endeavour that, for many participants, entailed intellectual and emotional labour in equal measure.

A second ISLDN study took place in 2012 which focused on the High-Needs research strand. Notman (2015) interviewed a sample of 13 primary and secondary school leaders in the lower South Island region of New Zealand. The research purpose was to see how school leaders defined a high-needs school as an organisation, and what they saw as key skills and dispositions for leading in a high-needs school context. Findings can be summarised under student, teaching, and contextual factors.

Student factors included the social and financial disadvantage of families, a higher proportion of children than normal presenting with psychological and behavioural issues, and low competencies in literacy and numeracy, especially for Māori and Pasifika students. Two major teaching factors emerged as evidence of a high-needs school. The first factor was a lack of professional development opportunity for teachers and school leaders, whether that be the result of inadequate funding or distance from providers of professional development. The second factor, of greater concern to the senior leaders, was the quality of teaching in certain areas of the school, particularly where it is difficult to change teachers' thinking and pedagogical practice to meet the diverse learning needs of their students.

Notman's (2015) study found school context factors were particularly exemplified in the geographical isolation of rural schools. Distance from major centres can create pressure for delivery of school curricula in terms of increased costs for services and difficulty in attracting teachers prepared to work in isolated regions. With transient adult populations and the attraction of employment opportunities in urban areas, some rural schools face additional high need caused by a falling roll situation, with its attendant problems of reductions in staffing, teaching resources, and range of student learning experiences.

In terms of identifying a range of skills and dispositions for high-needs leadership, the three principal respondents drew attention to the importance of focusing on the core business of teaching and learning, and on developing positive learning relationships between teachers and students. In addition, common skills referred to among the sample leaders focused on sound planning and organisational practices, strong levels of communication with the parent community in particular, and well-honed negotiation skills in sourcing requisite funding from government social and educational agencies. Professional leadership skills were required in setting clear directions and modelling the vision for the school: "Above all, there was a consistent call for high-needs leaders to have prior experience of working in a high-needs school environment or to have equivalent life experiences" (Notman, 2015, p. 40).

ISLDN methodology

The ISLDN research was replicated in New Zealand using the research questions and protocols laid down for the series of international case studies. For the Social Justice strand, the questions focused on what leaders in schools do to make sense of social justice, what factors help or hinder their work, and how leaders learn to become social justice leaders. For the High-Needs strand, major focus questions centred on how the concept of 'high needs' was defined in different New Zealand school settings, and on identifying key skills and dispositions deemed to be important in leading a high-needs school successfully.

Multi-site qualitative case study methods were employed for this phase of the New Zealand research study during 2015–16, using a total sample of 10 cases—three early childhood centres, one intermediate school, five primary schools, and one secondary school—to reflect the principle of maximum variation sampling (Maykut & Morehouse, 1994). The size of the institutions ranged from an early childhood centre of approximately 30 children to an intermediate school with an enrolment of 630 students. There were three male and seven female leaders in this study in a spread of geographical locations throughout the North and South Islands of New Zealand.

High-needs schools were selected against one or more of the following major ISLDN criteria: a high percentage of individuals from families below the poverty line; a high teacher/leader turnover rate and teachers not working in a content area in which they were trained to teach; a high percentage of non-native language speakers, indigenous groups, and students with learning differences. In the social justice cases, recruitment of research participants was dependent upon three factors. Firstly, in accordance with the international research parameters, the research focused solely upon the views, understandings, and intended and actual practices of school principals who feel a strong commitment to social justice. Secondly, by responding to an invitation distributed to principals of all schools in the Waikato/Bay of Plenty regions, participants self-nominated. Thirdly, the immediate and overwhelming response to the research invitation saw a purposive selection process employed, whereby researchers endeavoured to include experienced and novice leaders of primary, intermediate, and secondary schools, and women and men located in rural and urban areas, both high and low decile. While geographical proximity tends to simplify ease of access and minimise the costs incurred in conducting research, the research team deliberately included school leaders located a considerable distance from the university. This decision reflects a concern that diverse voices be heard, which is a social justice issue in and of itself.

Guidelines from the ISLDN methodology informed the development of a schedule for two educational leader interviews, single interviews with teachers, parents, and students where applicable, and the use of inductive cross-case analysis (Miles & Huberman, 1994). Accordingly, this book features seven case studies that inform a social justice theme and three that illustrate a high-needs setting in action.

An overview of the book

The rationale for this book is built around a research agenda that seeks to identify how successful educational leaders address social justice issues in schools and early childhood centres that operate in a high-need environment. The case studies chosen for this book reveal leaders' own reflections about their work, and underline the variation in leadership approaches and the differing contexts in which such leadership practice takes place. The cases are reported in different ways: some studies describe the leader's overall capabilities in bringing about a school turnaround; others focus on particular leadership characteristics; while another presents a narrative of a whole community's contribution to its school's success. The chapters are ordered by geographical location in New Zealand, from north to south. The title of each chapter captures the flavour of the predominant leadership approach and acts as a starting point for readers' subsequent reflection.

In Chapter 2 Cathy Wylie describes an inclusive principalship at a school in an Auckland inner suburb. This primary school principal uses her belief in students' potential and her capacity to be inclusive of students, parents, and outside agencies to help raise low levels of academic achievement.

In Chapter 3 Rachel McNae and Sheralyn Cook examine a primary school environment in the Waikato where the school was placed initially under statutory management, followed by the appointment of a commissioner. This case is an example of courageous leadership in which the female principal uses a strong work ethic and relational skills founded on hope to re-establish positive relationships among students, teachers, and the local Māori community.

Christopher Branson and Lisa Morresey explore an affective leadership approach of an intermediate school principal in Chapter 4. Here, the principal makes use of her emotional intelligence to develop cohesion and collegiality among the staff of an underperforming school in the western Bay of Plenty.

In Chapter 5 Deborah Fraser's case is also situated in the Bay of Plenty. She describes a primary senior teacher who is not willing to engage in deficit thinking about her students, and who develops opportunities for students to explore and question issues of injustice in real-life settings.

Michele Morrison in Chapter 6 reports on the case of a decile 1 Gisborne primary school. In order to overcome high transience and social disadvantage of the school community, the principal fosters student cultural and geographical identity and works hard to build student independence and resilience.

In Chapter 7 Mere Berryman and Zac Anderson adopt a different lens in their case study of a secondary school on the East Coast of the North Island. Their narrative focuses on how a rural school community and its college build relationships of respect and trust, and engage in promoting learning in a culturally responsive manner.

The first of the early childhood case studies is presented by Jeanette Clarkin-Phillips in Chapter 8. She highlights the social justice values of leadership within the management and teaching contexts of a kindergarten in Levin. Shared decision making and the unconditional acceptance of families are the hallmark of the general manager's leadership practice.

In Chapter 9 Debbie Ryder presents the case of a faith-based early childhood centre in Wellington that is facing closure. While the leader uses rigorous self-review systems and encourages staff reflective practice, it was the centre's core values that are instrumental in strengthening parents and staff in their fight for the centre's survival.

In Chapter 10 Ross Notman reports on a Dunedin early childhood centre that is focused on a holistic leadership approach. Here, the centre's strengths can be found in the high level of parental involvement.

Its leader is driven by a strong moral purpose to meet both educative and human needs, and to advocate for children and their disadvantaged families.

Chapter 11 features another Dunedin case study by Sylvia Robertson. It describes a primary school principal who leads a contextual change from the merger of an intermediate and a primary school to a full primary school (Years 1–8). Change management strategies are particularly directed towards teacher professionalism, collaboration, and the principle of distributed leadership.

In the final chapter, the editors review a number of social justice and high-needs themes emerging from the New Zealand cases. These are examined under four topic headings: conceptual foundations; cases of leadership that feature successful strategies; future implications for leadership stakeholders; and a series of reflective questions for readers to consider in relation to their own educational setting.

Each case study chapter in this book concludes with reflective questions or a reflective narrative for the reader. In addition, there are suggestions for further reading listed at the end of the book. It is the hope of the editors and case study writers that the successes enjoyed by the New Zealand educational leaders here will inspire others to action in advancing the cause of social justice in our high-needs schools and early childhood centres. We talk about closing 'achievement' gaps for disparate groups of children, but there are also 'opportunity' gaps for us to consider filling. Leadership is not a place where we sit. It is about being and it is about doing. It is about making a difference for all students.

References

Barnett, B., & Stevenson, H. (2014). Introduction to special issue. *Management in Education, 28*(3), 77.

Bishop, R. (2011). A culturally responsive pedagogy of relations. In D. Fraser & C. McGee (Eds.), *The professional practice of teaching* (pp. 185–204). Sydney, Australia: Cengage Learning.

Carpenter, V., & Osborne, S. (Eds.). (2014). *Twelve thousand hours: Education and poverty in Aotearoa New Zealand.* Auckland: Dunmore Publishing.

Day, C. (2007). Sustaining success in challenging contexts: Leadership in English schools. In C. Day & K. Leithwood (Eds.), *Successful principal leadership in times of change* (pp. 59–70). Dordrecht, The Netherlands: Springer.

Fullan, M. (2015). The path to equity. In A. M. Blankstein & P. Noguera (Eds.), *Excellence through equity: Five principles of courageous leadership to guide achievement for every student* (pp. 45–54). Thousand Oaks, CA: Corwin.

Gordon, L. (2003). School choice and the social market in New Zealand: Education reform in an era of increasing inequality. *International Studies in Sociology of Education, 13*(1), 17–34.

Gurr, D., & Day, C. (Eds.). (2014). *Leading schools successfully: Stories from the field.* London, UK: Routledge.

Hallinger, P. (2003). Leading educational change: Reflections on the practice of instructional and transformational leadership. *Cambridge Journal of Education, 33*(3), 329–351.

Klar, H. W., & Brewer, C. A. (2013). Successful leadership in high-needs schools: An examination of core leadership practices enacted in challenging contexts. *Educational Administration Quarterly, 20*(10), 1–41.

Lee, C. C. (2007). *Social justice: A moral imperative for counsellors.* Alexandria, VA: American Counseling Association.

Leithwood, K., Harris, A., & Strauss, T. (2010). *Leading school turnaround: How successful leaders transform low-performing schools.* San Francisco, CA: Jossey-Bass.

McNae, R. (2014). Seeking social justice. In C. M. Branson & S. J. Gross (Eds.), *Handbook of ethical educational leadership* (pp. 93–111). New York, NY: Routledge.

Maykut, P., & Morehouse, R. (1994). *Beginning qualitative research.* London, UK: Falmer Press.

Miles, M. B., & Huberman, A. M. (1994). *Qualitative data analysis.* Thousand Oaks, CA: Sage.

Morrison, M., McNae, R., & Branson, C. (2015). Multiple hues: New Zealand school leaders' perceptions of social justice. *Journal of Educational Leadership, Policy and Practice, 30*(1), 4–16.

Mulford, B., Kendall, D., Ewington, J., Edmunds, B., Kendall, L., & Silins, H. (2008). Successful principalship of high-performance schools in high-poverty communities. *Journal of Educational Administration, 46*(4), 461–480.

Notman, R. (2015). Leadership in New Zealand high-needs schools: An exploratory study from the International School Leadership Development Network project. *Scottish Educational Review, 47*(1), 28–48.

Ryan, J. (2006). Inclusive leadership and social justice. *Leadership and Policy in Schools, 5*(1), 3–17.

Shields, C. M. (2012). Transformative leadership: An introduction. In C. M. Shields (Ed.), *Transformative leadership: A reader* (pp. 1–20). New York, NY: Peter Lang.

Shields, C. M. (2014). Ethical leadership: A critical transformative approach. In C. M. Branson & S. J. Gross (Eds.), *Handbook of ethical educational leadership* (pp. 24–42). New York: NY: Routledge.

Shields, C. M., & Edwards, M. M. (2004, November). *Who is "at-risk" and what can educators do about it?* Paper presented at the New Zealand Association of Research in Education Conference, Wellington.

Sleeter, C. E. (2012). Confronting the marginalization of cultural responsive pedagogy. *Urban Education, 47*(3), 562–584.

Weldon, F. D. (2012). *Evaluating leadership styles of high-performing versus low-performing at-risk schools.* Unpublished doctoral dissertation, University of Phoenix, Phoenix, Arizona.

Wylie, C. (2013). Improving learning opportunities: Why schools can't do it on their own. *set: Research Information for Teachers, 1,* 45–48.

Chapter 2 "Nothing great is easily won"

Cathy Wylie

Te Papapa School in Onehunga has around 240 students, predominantly Pasifika and Māori. It serves mainly low-income families within a gentrifying inner Auckland suburb. The school roll is volatile, with a high proportion of transient students, making it hard to plan ahead in terms of teacher numbers. In 2016 that resulted in higher than desirable class sizes (28–30 for some classes).

Not long after Robyn Curry was appointed principal of Te Papapa School in 2009, she "completely floored" a board member when she gave the board a report on student achievement. The board member commented, "We thought it was all rosy." Such concern for student achievement and honesty gave the board faith in the changes she began to make and their full support to make those changes. One senior school leader said that when Robyn started as principal "we sent our Year 6s away with less than 10% achieving at or above National Standards"; around 90% had not achieved the National Standards. In mid-2016 the school's careful tracking of student progress showed a substantial improvement: only 21% of all students were seen as being at risk of not achieving the national standard by the end of the year in maths, 27% in reading, and 34% in writing. Its 2014 Education

Review Office (ERO) review resulted in it achieving ERO's highest level, a 4–5-year review return.

How had Robyn's leadership led to this turnaround? What teaching practices and school culture underpin increasing student performance in a school serving families who often have insecurity of housing and work?

What Robyn brought to Te Papapa School

Robyn was new to the role of principal when she came to Te Papapa School. She brought with her a fundamental belief in the students' abilities, and their entitlement to teachers who would have high expectations of them and see themselves as responsible for student achievement:

> I so believe in these kids, they have so much potential. I'm just sick of the perception out there that Māori and Pasifika kids means a poor school. They're not racist comments but they're just such low expectations for these awesome kids. Of course there are social challenges, but the only way to break the cycle is for our kids to have opportunity and choice, and the person who will make the biggest difference is ultimately the classroom teacher. (Principal)

> The school philosophy is: no failure for the kids. If the kids don't understand, it's the teacher's responsibility. With my older one [who went to another school], she says, 'I don't ask any more because the teacher gets angry.' I said, 'Why is this, is it just apathy or the work's too hard, or you're scared?' For her it was all three. At Te Papapa School they're eliminating that. If it doesn't work, they'll try something else. (Parent)

Early solutions addressed obstacles to children attending school, such as introducing a breakfast club; making free lunches available; getting support from the KidsCan charity for shoes, rain gear, and jackets; having a low-cost school uniform and some latitude around it; and no school donation. As one parent said, "The school doesn't give you any excuse for your child not to be here!"

Robyn also came with considerable knowledge of teaching practices that enable teachers to accurately identify and respond to individual needs so that students were engaged in learning that progressed them. She had seen the benefits of differentiated teaching in her former work with students with special education needs, including students whose behaviour had caused grief to both themselves and others. She came directly from a seconded advisory position with the University of Auckland's Team Solutions which gave her "fantastic learning with experienced principals, and cutting-edge research." These colleagues gave her vital mentorship and support with what was a demanding change process at the school. They worked with her to move teachers away from a narrow uniform programme approach, where "I got really sad to walk into classrooms and see teachers doing the same thing … All the children's stories would look the same," to develop teachers' capability in formative assessment. As teachers saw improvements in student learning, they became more enthusiastic about this approach—and their expectations grew for what Te Papapa School students could achieve. Putting students first meant changing teaching practices. It meant teachers paying much more attention to the evidence they had for student progress, and the effectiveness of different strategies:

> She gives free rein to teachers to work in their own style; the one
> thing she expects is that it's formative in practice and results in
> student achievement. (Senior leader)

It meant teachers working together more, discussing student progress in relation to what different teachers were doing, and it meant that school roles changed to serve this approach. When Robyn arrived at the school the teachers worked in two teams, each headed by an assistant principal. Teachers now describe a structure of distributed leadership, with roles based on individual strengths. One senior leadership team role now focuses on overall curriculum assessment responsibility, and the other on special needs and student behaviour. Both of these roles have been funded by the school board of trustees so leaders can spend time coaching and mentoring other teachers. Three team leaders take overall responsibility for a particular curriculum area and other key aspects such as work with families. They lead professional learning groups in regular cycles, discussing the evidence for student progress and whether strategies are working. They also lead the three groups of teachers working with the early years, middle years, and senior years of the school. The senior leadership team and team leaders meet each

Friday morning and identify teacher and student support needs, and one senior leader commented, "This is a very strong team, tight and consistent. We value our differences, the way we can bounce off each other."

Teachers admired Robyn for her belief in them and her challenging of them: her focus always on growth, whether student or teacher. They spoke of her leading by example, of being clear and passionate, always treating children and adults with warmth and respect, and being highly knowledgeable:

> I definitely landed on my feet coming here. I've really been set up
> for success in my career … it's not always easy but if you want to do
> a good job it shouldn't be easy. She gives us such opportunities for
> leadership, identifying your strength and giving you opportunities
> to grow within that… She builds your capability, challenges you all
> the time in your leadership, you're never resting on your laurels, it's
> always 'What can we do better?' It always comes back to our children.
> It's not about us, it's about the kids. (Team leader)

Board members saw commitment, determination, openness, and high expectations of herself and the staff to improve children's learning and achievement. One drew lessons for his own leadership role from the way she kept growing her staff and took their accountability for performance seriously. They admired her both as a leader and a human being.

Inclusion of parents

Parents felt welcome in the school and included in their child's learning. One parent offers an insightful glimpse:

> What I like about this school more than any other is the inclusion of
> the parents. A lot of programmes to support parents reading to the
> children, support for the parents to continue the children's learning
> at home, resource packs for exactly what they're learning in the
> classroom, so parents know where they're studying, what level they're
> at right across the spectrum, numeracy, literacy, the whole lot. We
> have a real view of their progress. Helped me learn a lot as well, how I
> can help my children.

Another parent noted that, while recognition of students' cultures was a hallmark of the school before Robyn came, she had added a much stronger focus on the children's achievement. Robyn signalled both her respect for parents and the role that their child's learning would play as the common language with teachers by opening the staffroom for parents to come in and have a cup of tea or coffee whenever they wanted, and talk to teachers there, and then by opening the classrooms to them to visit whenever they chose. Parents felt respected by this encouragement to observe their children learning and through the ways teachers worked with them to support their children's learning:

> My daughter didn't like maths. At the beginning of the year I came in and I talked with the teacher and they're like really into her with the maths, and I follow up, and she really enjoys it now. She says, 'Oh now I get it Mum and before I didn't, that's why I said I didn't like it.' Really good for me to follow up, I always come in for the 3-way conference, then I follow up with the teacher, about their development, look at her tests. (Parent)

Te Papapa School had embedded the Mutukaroa approach[1] to home–school partnerships that involve parents more deeply in their children's learning, with one of the leadership team sitting down with parents individually and sharing with them their child's progress, learning goals, and games or activities they could do with their child at home to support their progress.

Parents' comments showed enthusiasm for this partnership, the activities they did at home with their child, and the efficacy it gave them:

> That was another fear I had, how am I going to help her if I don't know what she's learning at school? But here they tell me what she's learning, how I can help her at home, I know exactly what she's learning.

> It's fun learning—if I had that I'd still be in school!

> I struggled in school, I don't know whether it was the teaching or not, but I don't want my child to struggle. So Mutukaroa has been really important, means I get to help her, not just the teachers.

Robyn's emphasis on the importance of home–school partnerships and high expectations for students saw parents invited to periodic

---

1 http://elearning.tki.org.nz/Beyond-the-classroom/Engaging-with-the-community/The-Mutukaroa-project

workshops to see what learning progression looked like and how it could be supported with strategies at home. A recent workshop had 35 family members attending, with both parents and teachers recalling the fun in learning they had experienced together. Another was aimed at families of students who were at risk of not achieving the National Standards. The teacher leading this workshop shared the patterns in what the students were struggling with, focusing on a few things with related activities that parents could do with their children at home, and highlighting parental agency:

> I refer to research, that the amount of words that a child knows at 5
> is the best indicator of how they do at 16. I say there's no reason just
> because you don't live in a big flash house, don't have a big car, and
> all the things that others have that your children can't be the most
> successful. (Team leader)

Establishing open relationships and high expectations for children's success with family also occurred through a transition group, working with local early childhood education services to identify children coming through. The programme involved more than the customary school visits by students before they started, and had included a professional learning group of Te Papapa School and early childhood education teachers looking at curriculum alignment to make the children's transition smoother.

Robyn also met with Māori whānau, with Tongan parents, and with Samoan parents to get their perspectives on how well the school was meeting their children's needs. From the meetings with Māori whānau came the setting up of a Māori bilingual class for Year 5–6 students. Te reo Māori is visible around the school, in the school values, and is used in class instructions. The morning school announcements on the intercom are done by students, and start with karakia. New students and visitors are welcomed in through pōwhiri, with students leading the welcome in te reo Māori.

Seeing that students going into the bilingual class needed more vocabulary and proficiency, the school has now included explicit teaching of te reo Māori in all its classes:

> I looked at a lot of schools around Onehunga, and this is the only
> one that jumped out at me. It's important for me as Māori to see

Māori words, pictures, something that says we're NZ and helps my child learn more about her Māoritanga because I wasn't doing that, but the school has brought in all that. She's learning Māori words, Māori songs, that just blew me away … my daughter has got a sense of belonging, of who she is, and we can build on that at home. That's tremendous for our daughter's education, for us. (Parent)

Tongan and Samoan parents also saw their cultures respected in the school, in the everyday as well as the cultural festivals aligned with their national language weeks. One parent commented, "Another thing we like about Mrs Curry, she engages with each cultural group. She tries her best to blend in: she dances, wears cultural clothes, eats our food." Several talked of the school as family, or as one parent put it, "The school felt like family, a community family … you can feel the unity."

Parents also talked of feeling personally respected by the principal, feeling her door was always open to them, and never seeing her ruffled. She knew their names, she knew their families.

Inclusion of all students

The action of putting the students first every time was applied to *all* students who enrolled at Te Papapa School. As a result, the school was both safe and supportive for a wide range of learners, and it had become a magnet school. It took more than its fair share of students with special needs, including students who other schools had deterred from enrolment or had failed to engage and build their capability. As well as seven students on the Ongoing Resourcing Scheme (ORS) or with high learning needs, it had 15 of its 247 students on the Ministry of Education's Behaviour Service and Support, and two more in the Intensive Wraparound Service. Thirty-five students were from families with Child, Youth and Family (CYF) involvement, indicating children dealing with stressful circumstances. There were 83 children on the Special Educational Needs Co-ordinator (SENCO) register. Since Robyn became principal, Te Papapa School has not suspended or excluded any student, in line with its commitment to inclusion and adult responsibility for student learning, and she commented, "We don't kick any child out. I would never do that to my child, so why would I do that to anyone else's child?"

Fully including all students at Te Papapa School needed a four-pronged approach by school leadership. First, the school provided differentiated learning that engages students and speaks to their strengths and needs (covered in the next section). Second, it had developed a school culture and values that built staff and student social–emotional capabilities and respect and support for one another. Third, the school developed strong partnerships with skilled specialists. Fourth, it tried to get timely and relevant support from government agencies for children and families. The first three prongs of the Te Papapa School approach were working well. The fourth prong was the cause of some frustration and pain because government agencies were not well geared or resourced to provide the support needed.

Building a respectful and supportive school culture

Te Papapa School was an early entrant in the Ministry of Education's Positive Behaviour for Learning (PB4L) initiative. All of the school's teachers have undertaken the Incredible Years Teacher Programme, which builds teachers' skills and strategies in managing behaviour by defining and recognising positive behaviour and building children's social and emotional skills. It has strong systems and processes to support positive behaviour as a result of it being a PB4L School-Wide school for 5 years. It is now a Tier 2 school in PB4L School-Wide, using particular approaches for the students whose behaviour needs individual intervention. One example that was working well was "Check in, Check out," aimed at children who misbehaved in order to get adult attention. Teachers and teacher aides periodically checked in with these children to give them positive adult attention, such as taking photos of the child learning and saying, "How are you going?"

Teacher aides—usually from the community—who often had their own children in the school were an important part of the school-wide approach. They worked closely with the SENCO and classroom teachers as part of classroom programmes rather than attached to one child, and were included in professional learning.

Interactions between school staff and students were warm. The students were confident and trusting. The school's values, developed with students and their community, are mana (defined as 'respect'), manaakitanga (defined as 'caring for each other and the environment'), and mahi tahi ('working and learning together'). Year 6 students I interviewed said they liked their school because "everyone has friends," "everyone is nice to each other," "we get to see the best part of every culture," and that teachers were "fair: we are one big family."

Student feedback on each other's work is a common element in the teaching practice at Te Papapa School. Students also spoke of helping each other by sharing ideas for writing if someone was stuck, and by not distracting others. Parents noted that the children were generally tolerant, and accepting of difference. Student views are sought and used. When it came to developing the playground, they visited other schools to feed into their identification of what they would like to have and why. Students are given roles of responsibility within their class and school and sometimes with other students:

> The kids that help him in his class, they have to keep an eye on him at lunchtime, like make sure he's got his lunchbox, doesn't throw it in a tree or something. He's always got a carer, who's one of the kids, not an adult, and I think that's cool because it teaches the kids how to care for other people. (Parent)

Partnering

The leadership team ensured that the school worked closely with a range of specialist expertise. Resource Teachers: Learning and Behaviour (RTLB) were in the school several days a week working with teachers. "We really see them as colleagues rather than people 'coming in'," said one teacher. One of these RTLB had been their PB4L School-Wide coach for 4 years. She and a Ministry of Education special education psychologist were part of the school's PB4L School-Wide monthly team meeting to ensure cohesion. They ran relevant professional learning sessions for staff, often with teachers and teacher aides together, or shared professional learning with them, such as a recent day on restorative practices.

Recently the school has had particular success with a small group of 10 children, working with one of the special education psychologists on a narrative therapy approach, where students write books with adults and choose what positive behaviour they want to have noticed. The book goes home to parents or caregivers, as well as being shared with adults in the school:

We were able to support that child to change the way he views himself, to change the way the school community views him, to change his reputation—between the work of this psychologist, his supportive Nana, and a stunning teacher willing to go that extra mile—a significant shift in the space of about 16 weeks from that kid who you had to ring Nana about 'he's on the roof again'— he was so angry—to one who had a better understanding of what he could do when that feeling of anger comes over him. He is not perfect, he still has blips—but he became a student counsellor this year. (SENCO)

Good relations with local police had also led to the successful 'police squad', building a group of boys' social and self-management skills so that they could turn away from physical conflict in the playground: showing how skills such as deep breathing, self-talk, setting goals, and visualising enabled police and Navy Seal teams to work through tense situations. This was followed up with a session with local rugby league players reinforcing these messages.

A part-time social worker has been invaluable, as has the local public health nurse. They too were seen as part of the school team, rather than as periodic visitors.

The enduring quest for connected support

There was further support that the children needed that Robyn and her staff found difficult to access. Ministry of Education speech language therapists were in short supply and often inexperienced. It had taken 4 years to get some counselling through CYF for a traumatised child. It was even more difficult to get assessments of children's mental and health needs and follow-up if children and their families were not under CYF care. Families who needed support that could come through CYF were often reluctant to approach the agency, associating it with loss of control over their family: "As soon as you get CYF involved, the families lose trust, they often pick up their children and run somewhere else ... even if I tell them there are whānau agreements they can have, that they're not out to uplift your children."

On one occasion, Robyn had called all the relevant agencies together to seek more connected support for the children and their families. However, each agency operates with its own service priorities and processes, and what she sought continues to be elusive. While she felt that the staff were doing well in addressing barriers to learning inside the school, it was harder to address the barriers students faced beyond it:

> I dread to think how many hours you spend having these meetings, fighting for the basic rights of children, how can they possibly access learning to the level that they need to, when those basic needs aren't being met?

> I say to my teachers, you can't use deficit thinking, you can't tell us they're not learning because they're not going to bed on time, or they're not having breakfast, because we give them breakfast, we let them sleep, we do all those things because ultimately we want them to learn, because the only way these kids are ever going to get equity in this world, is if they're educated, and they have some choice, so that's what always drives me, and to do that they need interagency work, they need this wraparound for all their needs, and they need the very best teachers. (Principal)

Robyn's advocacy for students and her core belief that every student's needs should be well met meant that the school had a strong culture and set of practices and partnerships to support and develop students' own agency. She continued to seek the additional support for the school's students and families, despite ongoing difficulties.

Growing the best teachers
Responsibility for the efficacy and success of its teachers is at the heart of the Te Papapa School leadership work and the decision to prioritise staffing resources for the leadership team to work directly with individual teachers. There is a collective approach to teaching practice:

> The model is that a teacher is never left on their own, so when they come into the school we put a coach in with them for part of the day, and then we make a decision on what kind of coaching it will be, whether it's talking with the teacher, whether it's the modelling, whether it's observation then giving the feedback afterwards, whether it's the interruption model—whatever fits, whatever is right for that teacher, but we work really hard to make sure that no teacher is ever left to struggle on their own. We try to identify really quickly where the support is needed. (Principal)

Care was also taken to distribute the students with high behavioural needs so that new teachers to the school—who were also often beginning teachers—had none or only one in their class. This was proving more difficult with the current number of such students.

Some of the hallmarks of the Te Papapa School pedagogy are:

- Intensive planning based on the evidence of what children could do and what they needed to do next, in relation to clear progressions. The planning was done every few days, within 3-weekly cycles checking where students were in relation to the progress they should make through the year. Te Papapa School teachers and team leaders had worked together to create clear sets of progressions in reading, writing, and mathematics based on national documents. Finding that the first writing stage was very broad, with students staying for a long time at the emergent level, the team leader described four stages within it, so that both students and teachers could describe progress and set specific goals.

- Fluid grouping of children, often changing week to week, and by their needs, not by their progression level. Children did not need to have achieved everything in a progression level to gain from being exposed to material and skills at the next level.

- Professional learning groups every fortnight bring teachers together to discuss target students as a team, think of different ways of doing things—which might include cross-class grouping—and report back on how well something new had worked. This grows individual teacher knowledge and confidence to be adaptive as well as the sense of collective responsibility for all students' progress. It had taken a while for teachers to see that the focus on target students (those achieving below the national standard) was not only for the target students' benefit, but would benefit all their students through their strengthening of their reflection on what they were doing and the impact it had.

- Tracking of student progress at the individual teacher, team leader, and school leader levels, and sharing of this tracking so that everyone can see what is happening, enabling the quick identification of any stalling in progress—or gains that could be inquired into and learnt from, and for leaders to have "these really challenging conversations with teachers" (Team leader). School leaders seeing patterns of progress across year levels over time could lead to fruitful discussions; for example, of whether in the desire to accelerate students, some knowledge or skills had been missed. "I talk about how it takes longer to bake a cake in an oven than a microwave, but it tastes better. You can't microwave learning" (Team leader). It had led to an innovative weaving of phonics work in whole language work that was resulting in much more solid progress for the early years of school.

- The encouragement of mutual challenge, on the basis of evidence, and seeking clarification. "It's important at staff meetings that everyone feels safe to challenge and question, ask for clarification— nothing should be about compliance, we should do things because it will make a difference for the children" (Principal).

- An increasing use of student goals, classroom walls, peers ("talk partners"), and teacher aides as resources for learning, so that student learning is not held up waiting for teacher attention. The Year 6 students I spoke with gave me some specific goals they were working on, such as "to read with purpose", "skimming and scanning to get information quick", "to hook the reader, otherwise they'll get bored, put away our story."

- Learning as play: resources that are engaging to use and chosen to advance the students: there is no 'busy work'.

- Weaving of literacy and mathematics learning into other curriculum areas, which often had a project focus.

- Explicit linking of school learning with having a good future.

- An increasing emphasis on students' capability to review their own work and have a 'growth mindset':

  Teachers help me to learn by always asking me questions about my work, asking me have I improved, or can I do much better. So I have challenging thinking on my work. (Year 6 student)

  We love the teachers and we've got the best staff members here, they push us, they believe in the growth mindset, so we do too. They support us. (Year 6 student)

Reflections for readers

Several students told me proudly that *Nothing Great is Easily Won* was their school motto. One of the things they believed in and liked about their school was that they were supported to keep growing and accomplish something that would not have seemed possible when they began. When they introduced themselves to me, they told me not just their names but, without anyone asking, also gave their ethnic culture(s), and what they wanted to be. Each of them could see themselves in a desired role, some of which would be new for their families: (in alphabetical order) a builder, carpenter, cop, news reporter, scientist, soccer player, and veterinarian.

The school motto also speaks to the staff and buoys them when their energy flags. The staff I spoke with glowed with the rewards of working with the Te Papapa School community students, and of working together as a supportive team in a school that demanded that they too be continual learners, innovators, and contributors, evaluating their own impact.

The hardest—sorest—challenges in their work came not from the students, but from the school context. Despite the school's high ERO standing and the achievement levels of its students, it was bypassed by local families who placed their faith in schools with higher decile ratings. The inclusiveness and openness of the school sometimes counted against it. The early childhood education service that Robyn had championed to set up on the school site did not see itself as part of the Te Papapa School community. The volatile school roll resulted in higher than desirable class sizes (28–30 for some classes). The size of the school made it harder to keep teachers seeking promotion. The intensity of the work could lead teachers who Te Papapa School had grown to seek other schools. Auckland's housing costs had also played a role in some recent staff departures.

Robyn and her staff did not gloss over these external challenges, nor were they daunted by them. Their focus was the students and ensuring they did their best by them. In our final discussion, with her two senior leaders present, Robyn asked me, "Where do you see the gaps in my leadership?" That question, in their presence, tells you much about the depth and strength of her leadership of Te Papapa School.

I hope that this description shows what high-quality and committed leadership can achieve for students, teachers, and parents and whānau in challenging circumstances.

Reflective questions

As reflective questions after reading this chapter, school leaders may want to ask themselves:

1. What am I doing to grow the agency and efficacy of my teachers, students, parents, and whānau?

2. How does our system support the development of such leadership, and the inter-agency capacity that it needs to support it?

Chapter 3 Leading turnaround schools: Surfacing hope in times of crisis

Rachel McNae with Sheralyn Cook

Introduction

This chapter illuminates the experiences of Sheralyn Cook, a primary school principal who led Taupiri School from a position of deficit to a place of strength. Over a period of 6½ years Sheralyn experienced the challenges and uplifting moments of leading and managing this school through 5 years of statutory intervention,[1] to being a growing, self-managing school. During this time Sheralyn's principalship was punctuated by numerous challenges. Working within a paradigm of hope, Sheralyn sought to engender a positive outlook for the future, believed that things could change for the better, and surfaced a sense of agency amongst staff and students. As she dealt with the messiness and, at times, chaos of embarking on significant cultural change, order and fulfilling professional relationships emerged from the transformation the school was undergoing.

---

1 A legislative framework comprising six different statutory interventions that can be enacted when the Minister or Secretary of Education perceives that there is a risk to the operation of an individual school, or to the welfare or educational performance of its students (Ministry of Education, 2017).

Reflecting upon her time as a school leader working under immense pressure to balance external Ministry of Education demands, teaching staff, student and community expectations, Sheralyn began to question whether her experiences and perceptions were similar to those of other principals working in schools under statutory intervention. This chapter shares insights into Sheralyn's leadership over this time and uses Snyder's (2000) Hope Theory which encompasses goal setting, pathway creation, and generating agency to examine the key attributes of her leadership as she led *in, through,* and *with* hope to turn a school around.

Background to Taupiri School—from proud history to troubled waters

Located in the greater Waikato region, Taupiri School is in a small rural village nestled at the foot of Taupiri maunga (mountain) and bordered by the Waikato awa (river), the Mangawhare awa, and the new Waikato expressway. The school has a long history of educating local children, dating back to the first Taupiri Mission School (1843–63), which was located on the western side of the Waikato awa. Despite flourishing in earlier times, recent levels of unemployment in the community, increases in social hardship, and 'white flight' meant many of those who had the financial means moved from the area, and this impacted significantly on the school and surrounding community. A falling roll, lack of community engagement, and burgeoning debt caused the school to become disconnected from its local community. Consequently, in 2009, a limited statutory manager was appointed to the school, who then appointed Sheralyn as principal. In 2011 the board of trustees was formally dissolved and a commissioner was appointed, who remained in this position until 2013.

In more recent years, the school has undergone significant changes. In 2012 the roll dropped to 18 students, which meant all students, from Years 1–8, were in the one classroom. However, the school was fortunate during this time to have two full-time teachers working in the classroom as well as two full-time teacher aides. The high student–adult ratio enabled staff to address low levels of student learning and achievement as well as work with the students, their whānau, and support specialists to address students' emotional, social, and behavioural needs. Deficit discourses about learners and their families were confronted, and new conversations founded on hope and courage ensued. With growing stability, a vision for the future, and the building of key relationships, student behaviour settled and student learning and academic achievement improved. Taupiri School began to gain a positive reputation for addressing and meeting the needs of the whole child, which resulted in a number of enrolments of students who were struggling in larger neighbouring schools. During the 2014 school year, the school roll dramatically increased from 18 students to end the year with 49 students.

Taupiri School continues to be a full primary (Years 1–8) with a roll of 54 students of whom a large percentage identify as Māori. The school curriculum emphasises place-based education, with the Taupiri local community as one of the primary resources for learning. It promotes learning that is rooted in what is local—the unique history, cultures, landscapes, opportunities, and experiences found within the Taupiri community: "*Toi te kupu, toi te mana, toi te whenua | Our stories, our mana, our place*" (Taupiri school motto).

Turning a school around is by no means an easy task. What leadership practices supported such drastic and monumental changes in this school? How might school leaders work with socially just intent to create significant shifts in organisational culture and amongst the cultural and social architectures? In this case, having hope and instilling hope in others was central to turning Taupiri School around.

Dealing in hope—leading change in a high-needs school

When Sheralyn was appointed in 2009 to the teaching principal's position at Taupiri School, the school was already under statutory intervention and the limited statutory manager continued to work with the school board to address the staffing overspend and significant budget issues. This was Sheralyn's second appointment to principalship. Here, along with leading the day-to-day running of a school, she would also be required to manage the demands of classroom teaching, identify and address the multiple needs of the students, the teachers, and the school community, all the while working with a school budget that carried significant debt. For several years this meant a grand total of

$200 annually to purchase learning resources, including resources such as art supplies and physical education equipment.

Upon reflection, Sheralyn recalls that throughout the appointment process by the board, her inquiry into the school's context drew some unusual silences from existing staff and the commissioner. She found it unusual that no one mentioned the poor state of the school financial records or campus, or the low levels of student learning. There appeared to be little concern about the lack of staff engagement, high levels of violence, and the extremely low levels of academic achievement. Not a whisper was made about the lack of community support for the school, or the teachers who were struggling to maintain their hold on learning and student behaviour. Upon arrival Sheralyn observed, "It was like all hope had been extinguished from the school."

The opportunity to reflect on her leadership practice highlighted to Sheralyn, and those she worked with, the powerful nature of what it means to work from a paradigm of hope, where hope becomes central to reshaping personal interactions, engaging in decision-making processes, and reconnecting the school with its community.

Working from a strength-based paradigm: Leading in, through, and with hope

Understanding the powerful nature of 'hope' provides a useful lens with which to examine Sheralyn's leadership for social justice. Ludema, Wilmot, and Srivastva (1997) outline four key elements of hope: that "hope is born in relationship, inspired by the conviction that the future is open and can be influenced, sustained by dialogue about high human ideals, and generative of positive action" (p. 9). According to Snyder, Rand, and Sigmon (2002), "hopeful thought reflects the belief that one can find pathways to desired goals and become motivated to use those pathways" (p. 257). Hope Theory draws together these key ideas and attempts to formalise some of these human elements defining hope as "a positive motivational state that is based on an interactively derived sense of successful (a) agency (goal-directed energy), and (b) pathways (planning to meet goals)" (Snyder, 2000, p. 8).

Following her appointment, Sheralyn openly acknowledged:

> We lived on hope each day. Hope that we could pay the monthly
> accounts. Hope that we wouldn't have any fights and any arguments.

I think just the hope that the kids would be able to see that there are different ways of dealing with things … that they didn't have to resort to the verbal, physical violence, or the emotional violence.

When voiced explicitly in these raw forms, it can be seen that hope can manifest itself in many different ways, as can social justice (Morrison, McNae, & Branson, 2015). According to Ludema et al. (1997):

When people hope, their stance is not only that reality is open, but also that it is continually becoming. Rather than trying to concretize and force the realization of a preconceived future, by hoping people prepare the way for possible futures to emerge. (p. 12)

Such a notion aligns well with leading a high-needs school with socially just intent. Most importantly, in this context, Sheralyn deliberately and intentionally led *in, through, and for* hope.

Leading in hope (of something better)

Sheralyn's leadership practices were underpinned by actions that generated hope for the future with both students and staff. She worked hard to set a strategic vision and collaboratively develop goals that reflected what might be possible for staff members and students, modelling what Snyder (2000) would describe as goal-orientated actions. She sought to broaden students' understandings of the world around them, while still respecting their local and cultural heritage. For example:

We weren't just a wee community whose biggest world extended to The Warehouse. The occasional child travelled out to Raglan or Kawhia … that was about the limit of their world. So I would be doing things like getting the world maps out and showing the places where I'd been, and bringing in the photos, and the money … just extending their world in that sense. I would tell them there's no reason for you not to go overseas, but if you have a criminal record, you will not be able to go.

As part of her leadership, Sheralyn saw her role as key to lifting student horizons beyond working in the local dairy or becoming the third generation in their family to receive the unemployment benefit:

I'd say to the kids—you know that you have the opportunity to do whatever you want to do, and be whatever you want … and I kept

> pushing that. I would tell them—you need to stay in school to get
> your NCEA … So have a plan, and keep coming back to that plan,
> and keep going with it. Ask, am I still going to be able to do this? …
> If I do this, what are the consequences going to be?

Sheralyn also noticed the teachers lacked hope and aspiration for their students. A significant part of Sheralyn's leadership involved reshaping the ways in which teachers perceived the students and their role as teachers. For example, she highlighted to staff that they were 'pegging' or 'labelling' new entrants before they had even started school, based on who the brothers and sisters, or their cousins, or aunties, or uncles, or extended family were. This behaviour was explicit and the labels were made known to the child, creating limitations that the child would particularly live up to. Sheralyn found addressing and reshaping deficit behaviour extremely difficult. It was most effectively addressed when staff left the school and new staff members were appointed. Interestingly, Sheralyn found it was easier to instill hope for the future in the children than it was to instill hope in the teaching and support staff.

Leading through hope (modelling hope and trust)

Providing a clear pathway framed within the school's strategic vision and goals was core to Sheralyn's leadership success. Described by Snyder (2000) as pathway-orientated actions, Sheralyn was able to highlight tangible outcomes as small changes occurred. She found this was critical in motivating and sustaining change within the Taupiri School context (for example, designing a new school uniform and moving out of deficit into a positive cash flow). However, not all changes were immediately obvious and this created a tension between the need to be accountable to external monitoring and the need to improve the social climate of the school. In some instances, the pathway became unclear and Sheralyn was required to rethink her strategic goals and amend timelines and the type of outcomes she wanted to generate. For example, she stated:

> I soon realised within the first six months I wasn't going to be able
> to really get any change the Ministry [of Education] would see as
> significant. I think the change that I got in that particular six months

was that the kids trusted me and learnt that they could come to me about issues.

Even this was perceived as a significant achievement.

Creating a pathway to turn a school around meant decision-making processes within the school were aligned to clear strategic goals. This was important because there were times when Sheralyn was required to make difficult decisions that were challenged. She found the ability to align decision making to a broader vision and framework one of the few supportive mechanisms for her leadership. She expressed the contextual nature of her decision-making process by sharing that, while decisions are made that for some people might seem unfair, for others it's the right thing for them at that particular time. She highlighted that decisions may not always be the same for everybody because a person's "backstory" needed to be considered.

Reconnecting the school with its community was an important part of this pathway and vision for the future. Sheralyn recognised Taupiri was an area steeped in Māori history and integral to the broader community's vision for the future. This involved supporting the students to reconnect with their whakapapa:

> A lot of the kids didn't know the history of their own area that they
> lived in, were born in. So within those first six months I was able
> to find someone who actually came in and took us through the
> history of the area … Tainui iwi, so that the kids actually had that
> connection. Because if they know and understand their history, they
> know and understand their place in the world, and their link to the
> world through their iwi, through their hapū, through their whānau.

As the school began to reshape its identity, the students were illustrating greater self-awareness and also formulating new concepts of themselves.

Leading with hope (agency and choice)

Hope began as something small and insular, a personal action that soon became a collaborative endeavour, which permeated the school context and moved out into the community.

Students were supported to develop the skills necessary to self-manage and take responsibility for their actions and emotions. Sheralyn actively worked with teachers to explore what this might look like in the classroom and how this might be a key feature of the school as it re-formed itself and began reculturing itself based on new expectations. Working collaboratively with staff so that many decision-making processes were shared and involving students where possible to inform change within the school was paramount. Examples of this included the formation of the new school motto and the development of the new school uniform. Sheralyn acknowledged the importance of involving the children in the change process and commented on how powerful a sense of agency can be for learners: "I would say to the kids you know, that we all learn from … from each other. That they are teachers as much as they are learners, so they are tuākana tēina… Oh, those kids taught me a lot." As hope became a critical part of the school's success, Sheralyn instigated further practices that sought to illustrate how others could also generate and work in ways that enacted hope.

Leadership learning—Sheralyn's actions and challenges of leading turnaround schools

Sheralyn acknowledged numerous personal challenges as she led Taupiri School through this enormous change process: "Being at the school taught me an awful lot about how much I can cope with, and take on, and deal with." The themes that follow contributed to her leadership 'in, through, and with' hope. These have been identified as understanding the self, understanding the context, understanding the possibilities, understanding relationships, and understanding compassion.

Understanding the self—having the motivation and desire to lead

Working with teachers and children in a high-needs school has called upon personal strengths and has developed skills and a level of perseverance that Sheralyn was not aware she possessed or was capable of. When asked what motivated her to take on this role she responded, "Because it just wasn't right. These kids had only got one chance at school … just the way that they behaved, just their interactions with each other. It just wasn't right. I needed to help get things right for them." In saying this, Sheralyn also acknowledged:

This school almost ended my desire to teach, and to lead a school. There were a couple of days when I physically could not leave the house in the morning, knowing and dreading what the day might bring. Yet, apart from those days early in my appointment, I have gotten out of bed each morning. I look forward to the day, of seeing the children (with all their behaviours, learning and social needs) and helping them to become the best learner, and the best person they can be, while they are attending 'our' school.

Learning not to visually or verbally respond to children's extreme behaviour or numerous parental verbal assaults taught Sheralyn self-control and a centring of calmness she could retreat to while holding an internal commentary of how she would *really* like to respond. The child, more often than not, had reached the end of their tolerance and learnt of no other way to let people know this. From her perspective it became her duty and her responsibility to help them manage their behaviours so that they could avoid this level of escalation in the future. The parents only wanted the best for their children and trusted that Sheralyn would support them to achieve this. Sheralyn felt it was her duty and responsibility to help teachers recognise the signs that identify the beginning of a child's time of crisis.

Understanding the context—having the insights to lead

With many members of the Taupiri community interrelated, it is not unusual for a classroom at Taupiri School to have students who are siblings, cousins, aunties/uncles, nieces/nephews, and whāngai members, as well as extended whānau. This occasionally caused some conflict within the classroom and across the school, as Sheralyn highlighted:

> Small schools, and small communities, they're interrelated. The children all live in each other's backyards. They sleep in whoever's house they happen to be in at that particular night. So they know what went on over the weekend … if a whānau's fighting … the kids are usually going to be fighting as well. So community issues come into school.

Sheralyn worked closely with staff members to support children in managing these often complex situations. They helped students to separate school and home issues, to identify their key triggers, to recognise when they may be starting to feel angry. The implementation of self-calming techniques soon became a daily part of Taupiri School's learning curriculum. Understanding the complex social dynamics within the community was an integral part for making change. Sheralyn elaborated:

> It takes time to find out who are the ones to go to when you need
> something done, or when you have concerns about a kid. Sometimes
> their immediate parent or caregiver isn't the person to approach. That
> there are times when it's best to do it via an aunty, or via somebody
> else—even though it's not the correct thing to do, it's the right thing
> to do. And knowing those connections makes a difference. And that
> takes time to build.

Understanding the possibilities—having the courage to lead

A core part of Sheralyn's leadership involved disrupting the status quo and challenging what was perceived as normal. This concept was highlighted to students:

> … that just because someone sees you're from Taupiri, and just
> because your family hasn't had jobs for a couple of generations,
> or whatever it might be. Or just because they're farm workers, or
> working in the piggeries, or the chooks—doesn't mean that you have
> to. You can go to polytech, or university. Get a trade and earn big
> money! You can do whatever you want to do.

Patterns of off-task, violent, and disrespectful behaviour from students were a key focus for Sheralyn when she arrived at the school. She was shocked that there was little focus on learning and students did whatever they wanted to do, telling the teachers where to go and what to do. Students' offensive language was commonplace as Sheralyn exasperatedly described:

> It was fully entrenched. They didn't know that the language that
> they were using was offensive. Imagine—[in] any other school or
> community that would be considered highly offensive, and they would
> be getting into possibly some serious strife with it. They didn't see
> anything wrong with their behaviour … within the school … 'Yeah but

we're Taupiri kids, that's how we behave at our school, when we're at another school [for field trips] we don't behave that way.'

Although the students were able to distinguish between two different behaviours and settings, they refused to address their poor language, arguing that it has always been this way. This entrenched attitude included students' general behaviour, and Sheralyn was aware that the older children were putting up major roadblocks to change, saying, "It's *their* school, it's the way it's always been done, so why am I trying to do things differently?"

Understanding relationships—having the commitment to reshape teaching and learning relationships

Paying attention to the practices of both teaching and learning formed an important part of Sheralyn's initial observations. She was aware of the significant impact teachers had on the classroom environment and noticed upon her arrival at Taupiri School how little time was actually spent reflecting on teaching practice and pedagogies due to the need to manage behaviour. In her leadership she highlighted the key role reflective practice could play in reshaping the ways in which teachers interacted with students and their families:

> There was a lot of time spent with teachers after incidents. So 'How did that go?' and, 'What do you think you could do differently?' And helping them to unpack that maybe they're also responsible for how things unfold, such as in the tone of their voice. We did a lot of work with the kids too. And also with new staff, learning about the tone of voice, and how that changes the situation quite fast, even if you're not intending that message to be—but the tone changes that message.

By supporting teaching staff to reflect on the ways in which they responded and interacted with students, the teachers slowly began to see the connection between their actions and the reactions they received from the students. This new element of reflective practice played an important role in shifting teaching practices overall, but also in reaffirming new expectations for student behaviour.

It soon became apparent to Sheralyn that not only did student–teacher relationships require addressing, but relationships within, across, and outside the school needed reframing and rebuilding also. Sheralyn spent the first 6 months establishing and building trusting relationships with the students, stating that it took time for the students to trust her, especially when dealing with behaviour issues:

> That I potentially might growl at them, or speak to them about their behaviours. But then once that was dealt with, it was dealt with. There was no 'keep going back over past issues', instead the metaphorical bridge was continually being rebuilt and strengthened.

Sheralyn adds that she kept stating to the children, "This is a new minute," or "a new 5 minutes," and "Yeah, you stuffed it up, but so what? We all do." Sheralyn explains that by not responding to student behaviour in the manner that they were used to, but in a dropped voice and with quiet calm, while saying, "When you're ready, come to me," and if necessary actually stating, "You will come with me right now," she role-modelled to the students and the teachers the expectation for how relationships were to be enacted within the school.

While Sheralyn found it easier to support students to learn how to build positive relationships with herself, rebuilding the student–teacher relationship was extremely difficult during this time, especially when staff did not feel the need to address their own behaviours or attitudes towards students. Sheralyn recalls a conversation with a teacher who had said something about a child that, when she investigated, wasn't correct. When she spoke with the teacher about this and stated that they needed to apologise to the child in order to repair the relationship, the teacher's comment was, "I don't need to apologise. I'm the teacher."

While relationships within the school were being reframed and rebuilt, parent/community relationships took longer to address. There was little parent and community involvement in the school. Sheralyn worked hard to reconnect the school with the local community. One strategy she employed was to seek advice on problematic issues. For example, she approached a local kaumātua who had previously been involved with the school, and asked, "Do you know anyone who could help us with the protocol for a blessing?" Through seeking his advice, she was able to reignite relationships that had diminished over time, and provide new opportunities for the school to reconnect with local iwi.

Understanding compassion—working with an ethic of care

Sheralyn displayed an ethic of care which was central to her decision making. The safety of children and staff was of paramount importance. This meant that sometimes Sheralyn had to work in ways that may have seemed counter-intuitive. For example, even in the context of a falling roll, she admitted actively discouraging new enrolments:

> … because we weren't safe… The kids were wild … we weren't teaching, we were just trying to maintain some safe-as-possible days, and really just getting through the day sometimes. And I told the board that I was doing it. I didn't think we were ready to have new kids. The kids were horrible to new kids, regardless of whether they were related or not.

For many of the students at Taupiri, the school became a safe haven—a place of stability, security, and safety. Sheralyn openly acknowledged that she worried about many of the children when they left the school grounds at the end of the day:

> My comment to them at the end of each day wasn't to have a good afternoon, or an enjoyable weekend. It was to be safe. That whatever they did, just be safe. I would say, 'Be safe, and make the right choices for you.'

This care extended beyond the personal and into the classroom where Sheralyn sought to shift pedagogical approaches so that they were focused on deep learning and developed independence amongst the students. She reflected what Wrigley, Lingard, and Thomson (2012) describe as deep care which they believe is central to socially just pedagogies. These pedagogies "understand the need to scaffold from where students are at, respecting their existing knowledges, while at the same time making available the high-status knowledges traditionally valued in educational systems" (p. 99).

Although caring for others was central to Sheralyn's work, she soon came to realise that caring for herself was just as important: "When you're really tired, and are just so focused on dealing with the minute-by-minute, the day-to-day, it's hard to step back." Taking time out to recharge, refocus, and rekindle the passion for making a difference was important learning for Sheralyn:

Knowing when you actually just need to take a day as a leader—just stepping away from the school. Knowing that whatever happens in the school, whatever the kids say, whatever they do, and whatever their parents say they will do, that it's in the heat of the moment, and while it can be quite upsetting at the particular time, or quite fraught, that it's still not about you personally. It's taken me a while to get to that particular stage.

She acknowledged that leading a high-needs school can be a lonely and isolating experience and it was important to know "when you needed support, or help for yourself to cope with a community or school issue." The challenge was not knowing who to turn to, or who to trust, especially when new to the community and to the region. Sheralyn commented that there were times when she felt a huge sense of vulnerability, and this impacted on her perceptions of herself as a leader. She acknowledged that things would not always go right and she described that it was hard knowing that sometimes her actions resulted in unforeseen consequences—both positive and negative. She also indicated a high level of complexity in the role of leadership with regard to remaining true to her personal values and beliefs:

> Being a principal requires us to be many things to many people, but above all, it requires us to trust ourselves, to be true to ourselves, to our values and beliefs, and to lead the school in a manner which we would be happy to work in ourselves, and to send our children to.

Hope-filled encounters—concluding reflections

In a number of ways, there was an element of serendipity with regard to the encounter between Taupiri School and Sheralyn Cook. A small, rural school, paralysed by accountability frameworks, financial demise, and community disenchantment met an enthusiastic school leader, passionate about making a difference, and brimming with hope for the future. Through this relationship and the changes that ensued, Taupiri School began to reflect what Smyth (2012) illustrates as a socially just school where:

> these schools regard themselves as having agency, do not have an overblown or overwhelming concern or preoccupation with their own self-image or self-importance, regard disadvantage as being

socially constructed … these schools are places of activism, [establish] personal rather than an institutional relationship where people's lives are brought into the school, [these schools] are listening organizations with a commitment to giving students, parents and families authentic voice in shaping their futures and how they go about learning. Socially just schools take considerable pride in foregrounding their mission of improving the life chances of their students, families and communities. (p. 14)

Sheralyn's leadership, which served to transform Taupiri School, reflected Fullan's (2014) argument that education has an underlying moral purpose to make a difference in the lives it serves, regardless of background. However, Wrigley et al. (2012) remind us that schooling is only one kind of education:

but its role is highly significant; it can either bring about the domestication of each new generation or launch them on paths of discovery and liberation. It can either reproduce ideologies of subordination or provide the resources and habits needed to question and move beyond them. School structures and cultures, as well as patterns of classroom language and learning, can either reinforce social inequality or challenge it. (p. 106)

In Sheralyn's case her aim for the students was that:

they saw that there was more to life than just literally the little wee village that they lived in. That they *had* and that they were the only ones who *could* control where their destiny is, that they are the only ones who could control what they did with their life.

Sheralyn's leadership was founded on notions of hope in its various forms and asked what *might be possible* rather than *what is broken*? This provided opportunities for the students, teachers, and the Taupiri community to engage in the opportunity to recreate and re-form a school open to new ways of thinking, doing, and being. In doing so, Sheralyn illustrated an "enlarged capacity to remain open to possibilities, envision a future in the face of uncertainty and creatively construct pathways that can be embraced as people collectively seek to turn possibilities into reality linking hope with the enactment of leadership" (Helland & Winston, 2005, p. 45).

In her leadership Sheralyn worked in socially just ways to illustrate the powerful nature of hope and what it means to be *hope-filled*, as she sought to enact socially just leadership in her school.

Questions for readers

- What activities do you engage in within your context to evidence your work for social justice?
- How does hope manifest itself in your organisation?
- What are your hopes for your school/kura/centre and how might you share these in productive and deliberate ways?
- What challenges/tensions of practice do you encounter in your context as you seek to practise socially just educational leadership? How might these be overcome?
- What might be some of the other complexities school leaders face when leading turnaround schools?
- What advice would you give to a school leader who was embarking on leading a significant cultural shift within their organisation/school/kura/centre?

References

Fullan, M. (2014). *The principal: Three keys to maximizing impact*. San Francisco, CA: Jossey-Bass.

Helland, M., & Winston, B. (2005). Towards a deeper understanding of hope and leadership. *Journal of Leadership and Organizational Studies, 12*(2), 42–54.

Ludema, J. D., Wilmot, T. B., & Srivastva, S. (1997). Organisational hope: Reaffirming the constructive task of social and organizational inquiry. *Human Relations, 50*(8), 1015–1053.

Morrison, M., McNae, R., & Branson, C. M. (2015). Multiple hues: New Zealand school leaders' perceptions of social justice. *Journal of Educational Leadership, Policy and Practice, 30*(1), 4–16.

Smyth, J. (2012). The socially just school and critical pedagogies in communities put at a disadvantage. *Critical Studies in Education, 53*(1), 9–18.

Snyder, C. (2000). Hypothesis: There is hope. In C. R. Snyder (Ed.), *Handbook of hope* (pp. 3–21). New York, NY: Academic Press.

Snyder, C. R., Rand, K. L., & Sigmon, D. R. (2002). Hope theory: A member of the positive psychology family. In C. R. Snyder & S. Lopez (Eds.), *Handbook of positive psychology* (pp. 257–276). New York, NY: Oxford University Press.

Wrigley, T., Lingard, B., & Thomson, P. (2012). Pedagogies of transformation: Keeping hope alive in troubled times. *Critical Studies in Education*, *53*(1), 95–108.

Chapter 4 Affective leadership: An illustration of the emotional side of social justice leadership

Christopher M. Branson with Lisa Morresey

Introduction

According to the view of a contributing school principal, the intermediate school to which Lisa Morresey was appointed as principal in 2010 was referred to as 'The Bully Zone'. Indeed, the SWOT data gathered from the teachers at the time of Lisa's appointment reinforced the appropriateness of this view. It highlighted numerous serious issues, including a divided staff, very poorly maintained facilities, regular instances of student overt aggression and violence, and the presence of a number of students who continually lacked respect for people, property, and school rules. Not surprisingly, the school enrolment was decreasing, student achievement levels were well below national expectations, parental involvement was limited, and staff morale was low. In this situation, coercive justice flourished whereby the oppressive and suppressive behaviour of a few students was clearly detrimental to the academic, physical, emotional, cultural, and spiritual development of many of their peers. Arguably, social injustice was becoming the hallmark of the school.

This chapter provides an insight into how Lisa worked with others to turn this underperforming school around. In doing so, this chapter will not only describe the effective but also the affective side of her leadership for social justice. It will illustrate how the effectiveness of the practical and logistical aspects of her leadership actions were reinforced by her corresponding emotional attachment to what she was doing and how she openly and naturally expressed these emotions. In this way, this chapter adds a unique contribution to the small but growing body of research literature that acknowledges the important persuasive influence of a leader's emotional state in successfully gaining the engagement of others during a difficult organisational change (Lee, Stajkovic, & Cho, 2011; Sadri, Weber, & Gentry, 2011; Tee, 2015; Venus, Stam, & van Knippenberg, 2013).

Contextual information

Mount Maunganui Intermediate School is an urban intermediate school located in Tauranga City, Bay of Plenty. It is an English-medium school, with one bilingual class established in 2014, and a U6 contributing school catering specifically for the needs of emerging adolescence in Years 7 and 8. Also, it is a decile 6 school and the 2016 enrolment totalled 628 students, including eight international students, and drew students from Mount Maunganui and Papamoa. Although there are four main contributing schools, the enrolments come from nearly 30 different schools and, due to increasing enrolments, an enrolment scheme was put in place in term one of 2016. While the school's demographics vary annually, the school is predominantly a bicultural school with 61% NZ European/Pākehā and 31% Māori, with a relatively small but increasing Asian population. Most of the Māori students hail from Ngai Te Rangi iwi. In 2016 this was 13% of the school's Māori tamariki, but the percentages can be as high as 25% of the total Māori students. In 2016 Ngai Te Rangi, followed by Ngāpuhi and Tainui, form the school community's biggest tribal connections. A small proportion of around 20 students identify as Pasifika, and a handful identify as both Māori and Pasifika.

Although these current data present a relatively positive picture of the school, this was not the case when Lisa was appointed. For example, on 13 September 2010, the *Bay of Plenty Times*, when presenting and criticising the misuse of 'stand-downs' and 'suspensions' by schools for dealing with student misbehaviour, publicly claimed that "Mount Maunganui Intermediate had the highest standardised rate for stand-downs [in the Western Bay of Plenty], with 81 per 1000 pupils."

Given the perception of the school at that time as a 'Bully Zone', this very public criticism of its attention to student behaviour management would have further eroded its public reputation. Moreover, it could have emboldened the bullies by providing public recognition and, thereby, some form of notoriety for their antisocial behaviour. However, the following data show how well the school community has striven to redress this serious issue since this article was published. In 2010, 4.32% of the students were stood down due to inappropriate behaviour, but by 2014 this had been reduced to 1.1% of the total student population.

Although the change in these stand-down figures is pleasing, as they point to the likely presence of a far more successful student behaviour management system now operating in the school, they do not, in themselves, automatically indicate that the school's public reputation has been repaired. To this end, the following student enrolment data provide confidence in the claim that the school is now very highly regarded in its local community. In 2011 the total student enrolment was close to 400 students and, although there was a slight reduction in 2012, this figure has significantly increased each subsequent year so that it now exceeds 600 students.

While these stand-down and enrolments figures provide reassurance and confidence that the school is heading in the right direction from the parents' perspective, they do not explicitly illustrate the specific cause of these very positive changes. However, the student achievement data do. These data show that the percentage of students achieving at or above the National Standards in both writing and mathematics has doubled since 2011. The key insight here is that Lisa's emphasis was as much on improving student learning as it was on behaviour management.

However, within the New Zealand educational context, the relevance of these student achievement data is somewhat deficient without more specific culturally related data. For Māori students, 64% are achieving at or above the National Standards for reading, 54% for writing, and 48% for mathematics. While for Pasifika students, 74% are achieving at or above the National Standards for reading, 67% for writing, and 74% for mathematics. It must be acknowledged that, as an intermediate school, the staff only has 2 years to work with the students before they move on to a high school. Despite this very limited period of time, the above data clearly show that the concentration on student learning is having significant achievement and behavioural benefits for a large majority of the students. Rather than the school environment being dominated by 'the bullies', it is now being influenced by a commitment to safety, learning, and achievement. The school has become a far more socially just community where each and every student feels supported in striving to do their best.

Clearly, the achievement of this far more socially just school community has depended upon the willing commitment and contribution of all, and Lisa is the first to acknowledge this understanding, but such community-wide involvement is founded on effective leadership. As Bolman and Deal (2008) argue, in organisations undergoing complex change the unequivocal need is for "wise leaders" with "high levels of personal artistry" (p. 435) so that they can inspire personal engagement and responsibility from all those they lead. These authors add that such leaders:

> need versatility in thinking that fosters flexibility in action. They need capacity to act inconsistently when uniformity fails, diplomatically when emotions are raw, non-rationally when reason flags, politically in the face of vocal parochial self-interest, and playfully when fixating on task and purpose backfires. (p. 435)

This form of leadership is as much about understanding people as it is about knowing what to do. Essentially, it is emotionally intelligent leadership where the leader is readily able to recognise their own and other people's emotions in order to use this awareness to guide their leadership thinking and behaviour. The following section describes how Lisa lived this understanding.

Reviewing Lisa's leadership practice

The genesis for the gathering of data associated with Lisa's leadership was the international research project seeking to explore how school leaders within a diverse array of national and cultural contexts enact social justice. Lisa was one of a number of school principals interviewed for the New Zealand contribution to this project. One of the important intended outcomes of this project is the formation of a more universally consistent understanding of what constitutes social justice based upon the description of it provided by those school leaders who are clearly committed to social justice. Thus, this discussion of the important contribution of the affective dimension of Lisa's leadership circles around her understanding and enactment of socially just school leadership.

Lisa's explanation of what constitutes social justice was simply, "I think social justice to me is not making excuses. There's no excuse!" The tone of her voice changed as she described her view on what social justice is. The first sentence was voiced in a more matter-of-fact manner as though it should be common knowledge. But the final three words—"There's no excuse"—were stated far more stridently, far more forcefully, and with far more resolve. These last three words came from not only her mind but also her heart. These words were entwined with emotion. Lisa did not just think this; she also felt it most deeply. She was claiming that not only should people not make excuses for treating others unjustly but also, and perhaps more importantly, she would never be able to excuse herself if she acted unjustly towards others. The emotion attached to her words showed the sheer depth of her conviction and commitment to social justice.

A tangible enactment of Lisa's commitment to not making excuses was reflected immediately in how she viewed her school on appointment. As has been described earlier, a view held in the general community was that the school was an out of control 'Bully Zone' where, if possible, parents should avoid enrolling their children. However, Lisa's initial thoughts on being appointed principal were, "somebody needed to love this place." Moreover, while some argued that the staff had not been doing enough to overcome the school's bad reputation, Lisa thought that "the school was really struggling" and so "it was a pretty sad place." In Lisa's opinion the school was not a bad place where nothing good was happening, but rather it was a place where things were being tried but these were not successful and so the school community was "struggling." The school community was attempting to redress its problems but it could not find the right ways to do it. The emotional side to Lisa's views in this regard became clearer when she said that because "some student behaviour was appalling" the staff "were very disillusioned but incredibly resilient." Moreover, although she did describe some student behaviour as "appalling" her general opinion of each and every student was that "they're beautiful kids here but the school was feral." Clearly, right from the very beginning of her appointment as principal of the school Lisa felt very empathically attached to the staff, students, and parents. She felt "sad" for the school community because she could see the good in all despite the presence of some inappropriate or ineffective social and professional behaviour.

The simple vision that Lisa had to guide her and the school community in the first year of her principalship contained both a practical and an emotional focus—"making the school a safe, happy place." When asked to provide some elaboration upon this vision, Lisa added:

> The child's the heart of the matter—that's very real for me. I love kids.
> I love their personalities, I love what makes them tick and … so every
> child deserves to have a difference made for them every single day.

At its most fundamental level, Lisa's vision for her school is not about behavioural control or academic success, but rather about a far more emotive aim of making a positive difference in the life of each and every child. This aim became more pronounced when she added, "But actually at the end of the day we need happy, safe kids who are learning—that's our responsibility and I don't care how we get that." Moreover, the depth of Lisa's conviction about the unequivocal interdependence of the learning (practical) and the happy/safe (emotional) dimensions of socially just education was based upon her "love" of the "kids" and their "personalities." Again, Lisa's emotional attachment to what she wishes to achieve through her leadership comes to the fore.

However, her emotional attachment, no matter how strong, would not automatically translate this ideal into a reality because it depended upon the involvement of resilient but disillusioned staff in order to make it happen. Previous failures can often create resistance to new ideas for fear of failing again. Despite this potential obstacle, Lisa commenced her process of educational change with the optimistic view that "you could change the world one kid at a time and you could change a school one team of teachers at a time." The general professional implication of this view for the staff was described by her as "every kid needs to be loved and as a teacher you've got a professional responsibility to do that." Specifically, this draws each teacher towards "having the relationship [with each of their students] to go—we'll find a way, we'll get you there, we'll find a way." Lisa's challenge to her staff is, "Who's really passionate … it's about—'are you passionate, you know, do you love kids, are you hard-working'—and if you're one of those people then come and play." Lisa's use of the word "play" provides insight into how she enacts her leadership. It shows that she is not about explicit micro-management, control, manipulation, or direction, but rather about creating the opportunity for her staff to work collaboratively together—like children who play together—to enjoy finding new knowledge about what they are doing and about themselves. She described her way of helping the staff to bring about the required changes involved:

> Collaborative planning just with a little group of colleagues to talk
> about—'Oh my goodness, what's going on?' And they join you,
> you know, come and play with me, you know? And so that's been
> something that I've really been working hard on, trying to inspire
> staff here, but then bringing people on that want to come and play.

Her use of the word "play" encompasses both a psychological and a physical dimension in not only the motivation to act but also the action required and the outcome achieved.

The pragmatic aspect of this commitment to "play" was about creating and maintaining expectations. Lisa's message to her school community was that the "students need really clear expectations, they need high expectations, and they need to know it's not the severity of a consequence, it's the certainty of it. So we had to build expectation." In other words, overcoming the impression that the school was a bully zone and the students were underachieving was not about clinically controlling the students' behaviour but "working with the kids around expectations, consequences, rewards." According to Lisa, the students desperately needed a learning environment where:

> they need to feel that they belong, they need consistency, they need
> to know this is the expectation and it's not going to shift. They need
> consequences if they're unable to reach expectations that are fair and

just. They need positive reinforcement when they do get it right. And, just that relationship thing.

However, in order to achieve this learning environment, Lisa also acknowledged the importance of working with the staff around maintaining expectations because:

> your biggest frustration is inconsistency, so building the [staff] knowledge base around why this aspect of behaviour, why we need to do this but why we need to do it collectively and where the inconsistency comes from and you can't just blame each other for the inconsistency, you've got to do something about it.

Importantly, Lisa added, "So we're doing lots of talking about what is expected but actually it's not me that has to enforce that—this is our collective norms and shared values." Clearly, the essence of the educational changes that Lisa led was about character building rather than behavioural control because the individual (student as well as staff member) was being asked to take personal responsibility for their actions as guided by community agreed expectations.

The challenge for each and every person was to "take a look in the mirror and, rather than blaming everybody else, what are you going to do differently one thing at a time to change the way things are here." Arguably, Lisa applied this to her own leadership perhaps even more than she expected others to apply it to themselves. Seeing yourself in a mirror evokes an affective as well as an effective response. You do not just see your physical self but you also develop a feeling about what you see. Lisa was inviting herself and others in her school not only to see what they were doing but also to be in touch with how they felt about the appropriateness and worthwhileness of what they were doing.

On reflection, Lisa recalled that, by and large, the staff "were desperate for change" despite "a lot of historical hangovers." Hence she spoke with sincere appreciation when acknowledging that "the staff have been incredible and really on board, and really quickly, but we've worked hard to get that." This generosity of outlook towards the willingness of the staff to take on board the professional implications of her educational vision for the school resurfaced later when Lisa added that "we put our heads down and we've done an incredible amount of professional learning and an incredible amount of work." But, again, these impressions were underpinned by a deep appreciation of the tone amongst the staff, the affective professional climate that had been created, rather than the practical achievements. At its core, this affective professional climate was imbued with 'relational trust'. A professional environment in which, when things seemed to be getting slightly off course, Lisa could confidently say to her staff, "In the interests of transparency and trust, and you know me by now and you know there's not a hidden agenda, we need to bring the talk back out in the open."

Although the essence of the educational changes overseen by Lisa in turning her school around has been described here in relatively positive terms, in reality these outcomes have been quite demanding. As Lisa admitted, the successful implementation of these changes:

> has really tested me and I know that when they appointed me they
> did a lot of digging about how tough I was—you know, does she have
> the resilience to do this—and I think I've been pushed to my limit
> but I also think I'm probably a lot tougher than a lot of people so,
> you know, it's that whole 'I think I can, I think I can, I think I can.'

Indeed, she went on to openly say, "I get really tired. I'm really tired at the moment. If I'm tired I'll get teary." The demands of leadership have an effective and affective impact—physical tiredness and emotional teary-ness—for the leader, too. More specifically, Lisa recalled:

> Probably the first two years I didn't really get a break at all, and I
> really did hit the wall in the middle of that two-year period and I,
> I still haven't got the balance back, so that's a personal toll I think
> because I like to exercise, I like to do things with friends, I have a
> husband who holds everything together at home, so I think that's the
> toll and the emotional toll as well so you get quite emotionally tired.

But despite this, Lisa recalled, somewhat to the surprise of herself and her research interviewers, that:

> I could honestly say like I have always loved the kids, I have always
> loved the community. But I can actually honestly say I was falling in
> love with the staff. I told them—you know I am immensely proud
> of you and so proud of what we all have achieved. I am actually
> falling in love with the staff. I think that was quite a huge shift for
> me, to actually feel that emotional connection to the staff, which is a
> significant shift.

When called to reflect on the totality of her time as the leader of this school, what surprised Lisa the most was not so much about the improved student behaviour and academic results, or the rapidly increasing enrolments, but more about the deep affection and appreciation she now felt for her staff. For Lisa, the hallmark of her leadership for social justice was its affective dimension—the love she felt for her staff who had worked collaboratively and tirelessly to turn her vision into a reality.

The role of emotion in leadership

In a general sense, the important role of emotion in leadership practice is now acknowledged and accepted unequivocally. Subsequent to Goleman's (1995) development of the concept of emotional intelligence, its application within contemporary leadership theorising is largely unchallenged. Simply defined, emotional intelligence is:

> the capacity of individuals to recognize their own, and other
> people's emotions, to discriminate between different feelings and label
> them appropriately, to use emotional information to guide thinking
> and behavior, and to manage and/or adjust emotions to adapt
> environments or achieve one's goal(s). (Coleman, 2009, p. 248)

When applied to leadership practice, the belief is that a leader needs to understand the cause and effect of their own emotions not only to ensure the appropriateness of their chosen actions but also to be better able to understand and work constructively with others. As described by Crow, Day, and Møller (2016), emotions play an influencing role in the way principals lead others through their relationships and interactions "since a key function of principals is to create, develop and work with school culture and promote and nurture teachers' motivation, well-being and job satisfaction and fulfilment" (p. 5). Hence emotional intelligence based upon the capacity of the leader to recognise their own and other people's emotions is deemed to be a fundamental characteristic of effective leadership.

However, the departure point of this chapter is its claim that there is far more to be understood about the role of emotion in the context of social justice leadership. Despite the lack of agreement on what constitutes social justice leadership, this chapter is guided by the definition proposed by Theoharis (2007) where it is taken to mean that the principal makes "issues of race, class, gender, disability, sexual orientation, and other historically and currently marginalizing conditions central to their advocacy, leadership practice, and vision" (p. 223). In Lisa's school, at the commencement of her principalship, many people—students, staff, and parents—were being marginalised by the antisocial bully behaviour of a dominant few and a seeming lack of resolve by the school's leader to do anything about the unsavoury situation. In a subsequent article, Theoharis (2008) describes social justice leadership as passionate visionary leadership because invariably it is made manifest through a "tightly interwoven connection between the principal position and the person doing the job" (p. 16). There is little that separates the person of the principal from their practice as the leader.

Moreover, it is argued that such passionate leadership "seeks to change people's beliefs and values from self-centered to other centered" (Theoharis, 2008, p. 16). Social justice leadership is not simply about changing behaviours and outcomes; it is also about changing moral attitudes and convictions. It involves bringing about effective and affective change in others. To be successful, social justice leadership requires the leader to inspire altruistic, rather than simply individualistic, motivation in others. To this end, social justice leaders must utilise persuasive communication instead of policies and accountabilities in order to engage the involvement and commitment of others to their cause.

Although previous research on the motivational effectiveness of a leader's persuasive communication (see, for example, Grant & Hofmann, 2011) and the effectiveness of a leader's charismatic presentation (see, for example, Awamleh & Gardner, 1999; Kirkpatrick & Locke, 1996) remains somewhat scarce and inconclusive, there is a growing body of research-informed literature that focuses on the influence of the leader's emotional displays upon their leadership effectiveness (see, for example, Lee et al., 2011; Sadri et al., 2011; Tee, 2015; Venus et al., 2013). Indeed, the research of Venus et al. (2013) found that when a leader's verbal communication is accompanied by a suitably aligned emotional display, the emotion is the more likely source of primary influence on others.

The role of emotion as an essential element of the social justice leader's persuasive communication is accentuated by research in the area of moral reasoning. Here, as Greenspan (2011) argues, the authentic and acceptable emotions of the leader serve as a rational barrier to any potential discounting reasons in the minds of others. It is far easier to discount a purely rational call to act in a desired moral way than it is when the call is accompanied by understandable and credulous emotion. The alignment of understandable and credulous emotion can significantly enhance a leader's verbal moral reasoning to the point where others are not able to discount or ignore the plea. This is because the inclusion of emotion not only creates a sense of urgency but also a sense of clarity. It creates a sense that the issue is so important that any delay is unacceptable while simultaneously creating a sense of transparency about what is fundamentally wrong.

The final contribution that emotion can play in the successful enactment of social justice leadership is in its capacity to contribute to building the cohesion and collegiality of the whole group. This contribution is said to occur in two important ways. First, social justice leadership is founded upon empathic emotion defined as "the ability to understand what others are feeling in order to be effective" (Sadri et al., 2011, p. 818). Importantly, this empathic emotion is not only associated with those deemed to be marginalised but also for those who need to bring about the desired changes. An effective social justice leader is considerate of, and sensitive to, the reality and needs of everyone, including those they are leading. In other words, through empathic emotion the social justice leader becomes very attached to those they are leading.

Secondly, when a leader displays understandable and credulous emotion this is shared across the group they are leading. The group members not only recognise the emotion but to a certain degree they feel the emotion. Furthermore, research shows that "shared emotion helps provide a sense of solidarity, forms an important part of group identity, and motivates collective action tendencies" (Tee, 2015, p. 664). Group cohesion and collegiality can be strengthened by the leader's display of appropriate emotion during key moments of persuasive communication.

These insights provided by the research literature into the important role played by emotion within social justice leadership are now used to help interpret how Lisa was able to mobilise her school community to turn the underperforming school around.

Reflections for the reader

Clearly, Lisa's data epitomise all that is now being claimed about the important role played by emotion in successful leadership practice. In order to achieve the extremely impressive outcomes illustrated in this chapter, Lisa regularly displayed a heightened level of emotional intelligence. She possessed the important capacity of being able to recognise, and be constructively influenced by, her own and other people's emotions. She displayed passionate visionary leadership as she tirelessly sought to change each and every person's beliefs and values about the inherent goodness of the students and the school, and how this could be nurtured so as to come to advantage all. Essentially, this was achieved by persuasive communication imbued with authentic and acceptable emotion, which not only captured the school community's attention and interest but also convinced the community of the importance of Lisa's perspective. Then, finally, Lisa's undying commitment to an inclusive, collaborative, and trusting process of change, which was combined with generous amounts of encouragement, affirmation, and appreciation, ensured that the staff felt emotionally and professionally supported as they slowly but surely gained the knowledge, skills, and confidence to institutionalise the desired changes.

This chapter has provided an insight into how Lisa worked with her school community to turn this underperforming school around by means of both exemplary effective and affective leadership. However, it could be argued that the focus of the research questioning—school leadership for social justice—had the potential to bias the data and, thereby, the discussion. This view suggests that the importance of understanding the affective aspects of leadership is only so when the desired outcome has, itself, a clearly distinguishable affective quality. For example, in the case of social justice, as described here, where Lisa's leadership was not solely about changing behaviours and outcomes but also about changing moral attitudes, beliefs, and convictions. To the contrary, however, we argue that exemplary affective leadership plays just as important a role as exemplary effective leadership regardless of the context and desired outcomes. Research-informed literature has attempted to illustrate and guide leadership practice for much of the past century yet the sense is that more still remains to be learnt. A growing view is that the current theory of leadership remains deficient in being able to fully describe the practice of leadership. Our view, encouraged by the writing of this chapter, is that this deficiency will remain until such time that a holistic leadership theory, which encompasses and synthesises both the affective and effective aspects of leadership, is able to inform and guide the practice of leadership.

Reflective questions

1. (a) What aspect of your leadership work induces the strongest emotional response in you?
   (b) Is the cause of this emotion more associated with your needs or the needs of others? What evidence from your practice supports this self-assessment?
   (c) How might your understanding of this emotional response positively influence your future performance in this role?

2. (a) Who are the marginalised in your workplace and what are their most pressing needs?
   (b) What is your level of emotional response to this issue? What evidence from your practice supports this self-assessment?
   (c) In what ways is your level of emotional response influencing your involvement/commitment to this issue?
   (d) How might you be able to do more for the marginalised in your workplace?

References

Awamleh, R., & Gardner, W. L. (1999). Perceptions of leader charisma and effectiveness: The effects of vision content, delivery, and organizational performance. *The Leadership Quarterly, 10*(3), 345–373.

Bolman, L. G., & Deal, T. E. (2008). *Reframing organizations: Artistry, choice, and leadership*. San Francisco, CA: Jossey-Bass.

Coleman, A. (2009). *A dictionary of psychology* (3rd ed.). Oxford, UK: Oxford University Press.

Crow, G., Day, C., & Møller, J. (2016). Framing research on school principals' identities. *International Journal of Leadership in Education*. doi: 10.1080/13603124.2015.1123299

Goleman, D. (1995). *Emotional intelligence: Why it can matter more than IQ.* New York, NY: Bantam Books.

Grant, A. M., & Hofmann, D. A. (2011). Outsourcing inspiration: The performance effects of ideological messages from leaders and beneficiaries. *Organizational Behavior and Human Decision Processes, 116*(2), 173–187.

Greenspan, P. (2011). Craving the right: Emotions and moral reasons. In C. Bagnoli (Ed.), *Morality and the emotions* (pp. 39–61). New York, NY: Oxford University Press.

Kirkpatrick, S. A., & Locke, E. A. (1996). Direct and indirect effects of three core charismatic leadership components on performance and attitudes. *Journal of Applied Psychology, 81*(1), 36–51.

Lee, D., Stajkovic, A. D., & Cho, B. (2011). Interpersonal trust and emotion as antecedents of cooperation: Evidence from Korea. *Journal of Applied Social Psychology, 41*(7), 1603–1631.

Sadri, G., Weber, T. J., & Gentry, W. A. (2011). Empathic emotion and leadership performance: An empirical analysis across 38 countries. *The Leadership Quarterly, 22*(5), 818–830. doi: 10.1016/j.leaqua.2011.07.005

Tee, E. Y. J. (2015). The emotional link: Leadership and the role of implicit and explicit emotional contagion processes across multiple organizational levels. *The Leadership Quarterly, 26*(4), 654–670.

Theoharis, G. (2007). Social justice educational leaders and resistance: Toward a theory of social justice leadership. *Educational Administration Quarterly, 43*(2), 221–258.

Theoharis, G. (2008). Woven in deeply: Identity and leadership of urban social justice principals. *Education and Urban Society, 41*(1), 3–25.

Venus, M., Stam, D., & van Knippenberg, D. (2013). Leader emotion as a catalyst of effective leader communication of visions, value-laden messages, and goals. *Organizational Behavior and Human Decision Processes, 122*(1), 53–68.

Chapter 5 Penny Deane: Transformative leader

Deborah Fraser

Introduction

Teachers who value social justice find they are increasingly constrained by external forces focused more on narrowly measuring student achievement than growing critical and compassionate citizens. Teachers do not intend to ignore social justice; they do so by default, caught up in the incessant demands of an assessment-driven curriculum. Moreover, some teachers are too easily captured by deficit assumptions about students who are judged to be below standard and lacking the cultural capital that breeds success at school (Berryman & Bishop, 2016). This chapter reveals how Penny Deane—a senior teacher at Omanu School—enacted social justice with her students. This case reveals layers of social justice in action—for her class, her local community, and for a community in Samoa.

School context—Omanu School

Omanu School is an urban primary school located in Mount Maunganui in the Western Bay of Plenty of the North Island. It shares its boundaries with the local high school and the intermediate school. With a roll of close to 560 students, a relatively large proportion (comparative to other schools in the area) of the school population identify as Māori (20%). As a contributing school it draws on a varied economic and social community, positioning it as a decile 6 school. With a school kaupapa founded on the notion of 'The Omanu Kid', students and staff champion innovative ways to learn and develop relationships in a positive learning environment (Education Review Office, 2013).

Transformative leadership in action

To understand how a project of such magnitude came about, it is important to make sense of how Penny used her teaching position and engaged with her students to work for socially just outcomes. For Penny Deane, social justice is not a frill or expendable extra that might be considered once the important work of numeracy and literacy has been attended to. It is central to her moral and ethical stance as an educator. Her leadership emulates transformative principles as defined by Shields (2003). First, she does not rely on traditional rituals of practice that may have served students in the past. She acknowledges cross-cultural communities of difference. This means she is "open to learning from others whose traditions and perspectives are different" (Shields, 2003, p. 3) from her own. Second, her leadership is firmly rooted in the rich soil of moral and ethical principles and her actions as a leader in the school and the wider community consistently reflect this. Third, she makes decisions about her students based on both social justice and depth of learning. The two are not antithetical despite what some might surmise. To promote social justice does not mean to accept mediocre work from students at risk. It means Penny questions who is served by school processes and who is marginalised or excluded. This includes everything from resource allocation to high-stakes assessment. Underlining her decision making is a keen sense of fairness. Too often schools perpetuate the status quo, privileging those for whom the system is already suited. As a transformative leader Penny realises teachers are part of the problem when it comes to disadvantaging certain groups of students and she deliberately works to redress this injustice.

A case of social justice in action

A Year 3 girl returned to Omanu School after the holidays and shared with her teacher stories of the devastation she had witnessed first-hand in Samoa when a tsunami struck, triggered by an earthquake of magnitude 8.2. She had been on holiday in Samoa at the time with her mother and Samoan-born grandfather. They did what they could to support the most affected areas, collecting money from hotel guests and taking supplies to the worst hit villages. The worst affected areas were in the north, including devastation to the villages of Salea'aumua, Saleapaga, and Satitoa on the island of Upolu. Satitoa School was completely destroyed and other schools were so badly water damaged that they were structurally unsafe. Events like this invariably touch New Zealanders deeply given the numbers of Kiwis of Samoan descent and the connections New Zealand has, culturally and historically, with the South Pacific. After the initial donations, aid dwindled and virtually ceased as is common with most disaster responses. Clean-up and rebuilding tended to focus on the tourist spots, but the destruction of homes, schools, and communities was basically neglected. Three months later in the areas less frequented by tourists it still looked like a scene of devastation. Added to this were heavy tropical rains making transport and rebuilding difficult.

Once back in New Zealand, the girl, the girl's mother, and Penny, the teacher, discussed ways in which they would sustain a support effort to help rebuild lives in Samoa. The discussion grew to include the class with the natural catalyst coming from the child's experience and her family's concern about the after-effects of the disaster. Media coverage also heightened awareness for the class of Year 3 children.

Thinking globally, acting locally

In negotiation with their teacher and the child's mother, the class decided to focus their support efforts on Satitoa School. The five-room school had been completely destroyed; all that remained was the concrete pad upon which the school had once been erected. Focusing in on the school enabled the children to empathise and connect, drawing upon their own experience as school children. However, research was required to piece together what was needed, as the teacher realised that the differences between the two countries could result in offering irrelevant or inappropriate goods and materials. The children's need to study the geography, culture, and customs of Samoa had a real and urgent purpose. The more they knew, the more likely they were to be able to make a useful contribution. Children's questions helped to frame their investigation and these also multiplied as they discovered more about Satitoa. These questions included: What do they need right now? What had they lost? What might they need in a few weeks' time? What sorts of food are best to gather? What clothing do they wear? How can we make sure that what we send finds the children who need what we have collected? How are the children feeling? Would they like some of my toys? What games do they play? Initial thoughts were to get a container and fill it with things that might be useful. However, they soon learnt that there was much more to it than that.

The children began to list the items required for re-stocking a school. These included school bags, paper, pencils, books, desks and chairs, shelving units, pinboards, whiteboards, blackboards, fans, filing cabinets, and so forth. They soon discovered that school life could not be separated from home and community life. Their research, with the skilful guidance of their teacher, enabled them to also list items that were required by the Samoan school children's families and community. As more information about the effects of the tsunami was gathered they realised the children and their families needed (amongst other things) clothing for all ages, basic survival and cooking equipment, tools, storage containers for food and water, recreational equipment, buckets, mosquito nets, rakes, brooms, and toiletries.

The class soon realised that to attempt to meet such a vast array of needs they needed to ask for help from the broader local community. Through a series of communications, including email, faxes, letters, and asking around, the class rallied the support of 16 local schools and kindergartens and a large number of businesses. The children ran some hard bargains with building companies and sought the best prices. However, they soon learnt that a number of places would donate materials once they knew what the purpose was.

Over a 6-week period the children successfully gathered the teaching and learning materials, games, physical education equipment, storage and shelving, pinboards, clocks, blackboards, stationery, art gear, cleaning and basic maintenance equipment needed to reopen the five-classroom school. Every child from Satitoa School was sent a new school bag with the stationery required for a year's education. In addition, one of the most touching things the New Zealand children decided to do was to send each child at Satitoa a care box. Discussion and debate ensued about what should go in the boxes. They decided that the items had to be useful and environmentally appropriate. They thought about what would be gender neutral as they did not know whether their care box would be received by a girl or a boy. They then listed and debated what might be welcomed by children in Satitoa. As these care boxes would go to individual children, they added a personal touch in terms of a hand written letter, introducing themselves and saying how they were thinking of the children of Satitoa. The care boxes contained items such a marbles, skipping ropes, puppets, toiletries, soap, toothbrushes, toothpaste, comics, sunglasses, and hats.

As news of the classroom's aid event spread, many businesses came on board, donating a range of goods. A parent donated an old shipping container in which the class could house and transport the donated goods. A trucking company then offered to paint and write a sign on the container to spruce it up. Pacific Blue Airlines donated three air tickets so that the teacher, mother, and grandfather who initiated the project could collect and unload the container when it docked once it cleared customs. They also worked with the Samoan Ministry of Education, the local council of Matai, and disaster relief co-ordinators to ensure that cultural protocols were observed and to guide the delivery of goods to the new school site. What had started as a child's observation and interest had grown into a significant project requiring multiple levels of collaboration, diverse networks of communication, and immense logistical management. Penny's work as a teacher was key to growing this initial inquiry into a collaborative effort of giving and service founded on social justice, shifting the impact from a local inquiry about a context into an international aid effort enacted and driven by the students.

The complexity of teachers' work

This case illustrates how Penny's teaching was informed through her work as a transformative leader. It also reveals the complexity of teachers' work (O'Connell Rust, 2016) and highlights the diverse and multifaceted nature of inquiring into issues of social justice. She negotiated the curriculum with her students so that they were part of the powerful conversation of learning, not just passive recipients of instructions. High levels of democratic pedagogy (Beane, 2005) were evident in Penny's classroom, as the children actively negotiated and developed the classroom curriculum. Fraser and Paraha (2002) point out that when teachers and students co-construct the learning process, there is a redress of power relationships. This can readily lead to enhanced motivation, relevance, and learning for students, especially for those students who are traditionally marginalised. This project drew and sustained its momentum from the commitments of the students. The connection between the students' desire to 'do good' and the associated curriculum activities that Penny facilitated required a knowledgeable and courageous teacher who was willing to trust others.

Penny's social justice stance has implications for the big ideas that underpin the curriculum. In her class, many of the big ideas (such as the Samoan aid project) are ones that speak deeply to her students. These ideas include fairness, justice, empathy, awareness of others, resilience, and resourcefulness. This resonates with Nuthall's (2007) classroom research which also revealed the importance of focusing on the big ideas in teaching. Wilkinson and Anderson (as cited in Nuthall, 2007) add:

> We need to focus on major questions and problems that provide the most pay-off for students … it is better to invest teaching time and resources in a smaller number of big questions or problems in depth, rather than in covering every aspect of the curriculum at some surface level of understanding. (p. 162)

It is evident from the Samoan project described here that Penny acknowledged and worked with cross-cultural communities of difference. This began with the Samoan girl in her class, and her family, and grew to include the local community of Omanu, the Matai in Samoa, the Samoan principal of Satitoa School, and the village community of the area. It is also evident that Penny bases her teaching on moral and ethical values. It takes immense moral fortitude, as well as persistence, for any teacher to embark on such an ambitious project with her class. As McNae (2014) states, "Leading with socially just intent requires courage and resilience, as well as conviction, for socially just leaders are compelled to be fully involved participants in their own initiatives" (p. 98). Penny's thorough engagement with her class, her community, and the community in Samoa was a total immersion experience for teacher and children alike.

All the students in her class, regardless of ability level, had real and challenging tasks to undertake. Moreover, as the project grew the children increasingly made their own decisions about what was required, working long hours to fulfil tasks for the project. This last point is salient; they did not work hard because they were told to, or because a test was looming. They did so because they were engaged, motivated, and concerned. They did so because their teacher and classmate opened a challenge to them that appealed to their keen sense of justice. They did so because they empathised with children they did not know who had survived destruction and devastation. In an increasingly profit-oriented, competitive world, projects like these are a timely reminder of the deeper goals of education. To educate the whole child includes their heart, their soul, and their sense of conscience. Teachers like Penny ensure these deep goals of education are not lost in the flurry to reach certain assessment targets.

Having said that, it became clear that numerous curriculum and assessment goals were achieved with this project. As Shields (2003) states, achievement is not antithetical to the goals of social justice. An extensive, integrated project like this draws upon many curriculum subject areas. In mathematics, examples included the measurement of blackboards and pinboards, capacity (how many banana boxes fit in a shipping container), time (international time differences, shipping dates, and passages), statistics (graphing to keep track of ideas and results), numeracy (keeping track of purchases and donations; counting in multiples such as 20 tennis balls per bag), money and problem solving (how many pairs of scissors does a class need, does a school need, what is the total cost and is it affordable?). In technology, students explored the use of emails, faxes, internet searches, and camera and video use for record keeping. In the arts curriculum, students examined and participated in the dance, music, and visual art of Samoa. Through reading and writing, students made posters to advertise fundraising, emails and faxes to and from local schools and businesses, communicated via email with the Samoan Ministry of Education, sent letters to children in Satitoa, wrote notes home and reminders, and scripted speeches. For oral language, the students hosted guests and shared learning, negotiated a bargain with various businesses, prepared thank you speeches, prepared questions for visiting experts (for example, Samoan family members, workers at Bunnings, when working with other adults on joint projects). In social studies, the students examined the way people have social, cultural, and economic roles, rights, and responsibilities, understood how time and change affect people's lives, explored how places influence people and people influence places.

Reflections for readers—students and teachers as change agents

A transformative leader like Penny understands that a social justice agenda needs to permeate the ethos of a school, not just a classroom. Individual teachers promoting social justice is admirable but for the underpinning values to endure, social justice requires more than the integrity of one or two teachers. Building a school-wide culture of social justice requires ongoing efforts to keep social justice firmly in the forefront of the school's mission. In doing this, schools generate strong feelings of belonging in students and teachers, their class, their school, and their wider community. This project was not a one-off event.

In Penny's room students have opportunities to take on roles as social activists (as well as marine scientists, mathematicians, artists, writers, and so forth). They pursue purposeful learning that is relevant to their lives. This includes exploring conflicting perspectives, mounting campaigns, and organising resources for communities in need. These respective roles gave them license to have a say in a curriculum that matters to them. Penny is not passive in this process. She is actively involved alongside her students posing questions, speculating, and provoking. In treating her students as capable, Penny conveys her high expectations of them and deepens learning for all students. She does not pathologise her students as incapable or incompetent and, as a result, is regularly impressed by what they produce.

At the time of writing, Penny's class ran a mufti day to raise funds for Fiji in the face of Cyclone Winston and the devastation caused. Another school in the area approached Omanu School for further guidance on how to support Fiji, which manifested in donations of school bags, stationery, clothing, and so forth. Teams of teachers and children packaged these goods to be transported in pallets to Fiji. Penny is mindful of the fact that involvement in such activities is not motivated by having their names in the news or social media (although this might happen). Such public attention is not a primary objective or a primary outcome. Indeed, the many positive benefits of giving are reward in themselves as philosophers and health experts have attested to over many decades. Giving has immense benefits for health and wellbeing. It also bonds children as they make decisions about the what, where, and how of their respective projects.

As long ago as 1937 the *New Zealand Syllabus of Instruction for Primary Schools* included an exhortation as important now as it was then:

> There still survives in the schools a great deal of the old-fashioned
> formalism that regarded education more as a mechanical process than
> as a means of securing for every child the fullest possible spiritual,
> mental and physical development. It is hoped that the present
> Syllabus will give encouragement to those teachers—and fortunately
> there are many of them—who regard the child not as inanimate clay
> in the hands of the potter, or as an empty vessel sent them for filling,
> but as a soul, a personality, capable of being developed and trained for
> the wider service of humanity. (Education Department, 1937, p. 65;
> as cited in MacDonald, 2016, p. 51)

This quote reminds us to honour each student's uniqueness and the service to humanity that is an ideal for many schools. In terms of developing competencies noted as important by the Ministry of Education (2007), opportunities to participate and contribute were significant. The children experienced first-hand what it means to be part of a community project, what it means to contribute beyond the needs of oneself and one's family, and what it means to support people in another country. Such experiences underline the moral challenge in education where teachers do not just teach subjects. Whether it is overt or not, everything that is taught is values-laden, and values underpin what it means to be educated. Again, the *New Zealand Curriculum* (Ministry of Education, 2007) is reflected in the project with its values emphasis on inquiry (into what was needed in Satitoa), diversity (in terms of Samoan culture), equity (in regard to supporting others in times of need), sustainability (in terms of ongoing community, village, and school life), respect (for local Samoan protocols), and contribution to "the common good" (p. 10). Developing understanding about fairness, access, and equity was an important part of this project. Values espoused in the New Zealand curriculum were integral to the work, as was the mode of inquiry, with Blackmore (2002) arguing, "equity is not a 'luxury item' but an essential aspect of a truly civil society" (p. 218).

Blackmore (2002) explains that active citizenship is reflected not just in exercising rights but also in "realizing responsibilities" (p. 218). The Samoan project provided ample opportunities for young people to be agentic citizens and take increasing responsibility. Even children as young as 7 years old can be fully involved in a project like this which expands their sense of responsibility and contribution; that enables them to appreciate their capacity to make a positive difference. In a school context, Beane (2005) asserts children deserve a curriculum that takes them seriously as change agents:

> The work they do should involve more making and doing, more building and creating, and less of the deadening drudgery that too many of our curriculum arrangements call for. We should ask that the curriculum challenge our young people to imagine a better world and try out ways of making it so. We should ask that it bring them justice and equity, that it help them to overcome the narrow prejudices still so evident in our society. (p. 136)

The social justice agenda that Penny leads provides children with deep responsibility, as decision making is vested in their hands. Young people in schools seldom have the chance to determine choices of such magnitude. A social justice agenda like this is kept alive by the everyday actions of students and staff. It becomes a way of being in the world, so that when a larger need arises, either locally or further afield, students regard this as their concern. It highlights their agency as social activists and it grows the bonds of empathy, so vitally necessary to sustain healthy and just communities.

This chapter has outlined the values and actions of a teacher who places social justice at the centre of her education philosophy, a need arguably more urgent than ever as society witnesses increasing gaps between rich and poor, greater numbers living on or below the poverty line, increases in violent crime, and rapid growth in prison inmate numbers. Considerable tenacity is required by teachers to sustain a stance on social justice when they feel increasingly shackled by forces beyond their control (Fraser, 2016). The work the class undertook was highly collaborative, socially mediated, and negotiated. The groundswell of support the students and Penny engendered from the wider community says much about the worth of the cause. Penny's leadership in this example shows that limitations are few and possibilities are many when vision, collaboration, and transformation are infused across a social justice agenda for change. It is through this process that both teacher and children learn and model to others that it is not too bold to imagine, and create a better world.

Acknowledgement

The Samoan tsunami story first appeared in *set: Research Information for Teachers* published by the New Zealand Council for Educational Research (NZCER). Permission has been granted to include that material here.

References

Beane, J. (2005). *A reason to teach: Creating classrooms of dignity and hope.* Portsmouth, NH: Heinemann.

Berryman, M., & Bishop, R. (2016). A culturally responsive pedagogy of relations. In D. Fraser & M. Hill (Eds.), *The professional practice of teaching in New Zealand* (5th ed., pp. 180–197). Melbourne, Australia: Cengage.

Blackmore, J. (2002). Leadership for socially just schooling. More substance and less style in high-risk, low-trust times? *Journal of School Leadership, 12,* 198–222.

Education Department. (1937). *Syllabus of instruction for public schools.* Wellington: Government Printer.

Education Review Office. (2013). *Education Review report: Arotake Paehiranga; Omanu Contributing Primary School.* Wellington: Author.

Fraser, D. (2016). Foreword. In M. MacDonald, *Elwyn Richardson and the early world of creative education in New Zealand* (pp. x–xiii). Wellington: NZCER Press.

Fraser, D., & Paraha, H. (2002). Curriculum integration as treaty praxis. *Waikato Journal of Education, 8,* 57–70.

MacDonald, M. (2016). *Elwyn Richardson and the early world of creative education in New Zealand.* Wellington: NZCER Press.

McNae, R. (2014). Seeking social justice. In C. Branson & S. Gross (Eds.), *Handbook of ethical leadership* (pp. 93–111). New York, NY: Routledge.

Ministry of Education. (2007). *The New Zealand curriculum.* Wellington: Learning Media.

Nuthall, G. (2007). *The hidden lives of learners.* Wellington: NZCER Press.

O'Connell Rust, F. (2016). Towards action and advocacy. *Teachers and Teaching: Theory and Practice, 22*(4), 409–412.

Shields, C. (2003). *Good intentions are not enough: Transformative leadership for communities of difference.* Lanham, MD: Scarecrow.

Chapter 6 "I wasn't really a decile 10 person": Deliberate enactment of social justice leadership in a high-needs context

Michele Morrison

Steve Berezowski has been principal of Te Wharau School for 15 years. This chapter focuses on elements of Steve's career biography that have attuned him to issues of social justice and the manner in which his leadership disrupts practices that perpetuate unjust educational experiences and outcomes for the children in his care. As the title of this chapter suggests, Steve's sense of vocation compelled him to seek a professional context that afforded multiple opportunities to exercise moral, professional, and political agency, and with which he felt greater personal affinity. Bucking the career trajectory that sees many New Zealand principals leading progressively larger and higher decile[1] schools, Steve relinquished his position as principal of a decile 10 city school and migrated north to the East Coast, to become principal of what was then a decile 3 school.

---

1   Deciles measure the socioeconomic position of a school's student community relative to other schools. Decile 1 schools are the 10% of schools with the highest proportion of students from low socioeconomic communities, whereas decile 10 schools are the 10% of schools with the lowest proportion of these students. www.education.govt.nz/

School context

Located in inner Kaiti, a suburb east of the Waimata River and Gisborne city CBD, Te Wharau is a contributing (Years 1–6) state primary school. While the school has an open entry enrolment policy, the majority of students live in the local community, which encompasses four adjacent census blocks (Kaiti North, Kaiti South, Outer Kaiti, and Tamarau). At the time this research was undertaken, there were 394 students enrolled, 85% of whom identified as Māori and 13% as Pākehā (NZ European), with the remaining 2% comprising five Pasifika students, one of Asian ethnicity, and one of MELAA (Middle Eastern, Latin American, and African) descent.

Demographic change during Steve's principalship has seen the school decile rating drop from decile 3 to decile 1. In 2011 the Ministry of Social Development noted that almost one-half (46%) of Gisborne/East Coast District residents were "among the 20% most socio-economically deprived in New Zealand" (Bull, 2011, p. 2) and that the poorest people were most likely to live in areas including Kaiti South and Outer Kaiti. The most recent census data (Statistics New Zealand, 2013) reveals that, in contrast to more prosperous areas of Gisborne, residents in South and Outer Kaiti continue to experience considerable income, employment, and housing disadvantage. They are less likely to hold formal educational qualifications, earn above the median wage, be living in their own home, and have internet access. A disproportionate number are unemployed, reliant on means-tested benefits, and living in sole parent families.

The social consequences of financial poverty are dire. Formulated to increase youth participation in education, training, and employment, and reduce truancy, youth offending, and alcohol and drug use, the 2013–15 Gisborne Youth Action Plan (Ministry of Social Development, 2013) identified major social issues affecting Gisborne youth. Against national averages, Gisborne youth were 200% more likely to experience reported family violence, 110% more likely to truant frequently, twice as likely to become teen parents, 73% more likely to be prosecuted by police, and 60% more likely to leave school without any qualifications.

Transience is also high. Compounded by a range of social, employment, and income factors (including movement of children within whānau or extended family, relocation to areas in close proximity of prison, seasonal work, emigration to Australia, and rent default), transience disrupts children's sense of place and their educational progress. In Steve's school a number of Years 1/2 children have attended four or more schools and turnover is substantial: "In 2009 we lost 180 kids to Australia … In 2011 we enrolled 281 kids but with only a 70 net gain."

In the face of these formidable challenges, Te Wharau enjoys a reputation as a high-performing school. The Education Review Office (2013) notes "a positive reporting history" (p. 1), staff morale is high and turnover low, and the student roll is rising. Steve's leadership has united the school community in pursuing their collective vision of a vibrant, respectful, and liberating learning environment in which all learners develop the skills and confidence to become responsible citizens, whānau, and community members.

ISLDN social justice research

We met Steve when he answered the call to participate in International School Leadership Development Network (ISLDN) social justice research. This research seeks to understand how educational leaders make sense of and enact social justice; what they do to expose, disrupt, and redress unjust practices; and how they perceive that contextual factors enable and constrain them in this endeavour. In New Zealand, research invitations were distributed to school principals in the central North Island region. The immediate and overwhelming response to this invitation suggested that school leaders welcomed the opportunity to engage in dialogue of this nature. The first phase of data collection during 2013–14 included semi-structured interviews with 15 participants and the construction of multiple case studies, of which Steve's is one.

Steve's personal and career biography

Born in Canada to working class parents, Steve emigrated to Wainuiomata during the early 1970s when economic recession prompted his father to seek employment in New Zealand. Steve was 16 years old at the time and had just completed the Canadian equivalent of Year 11. Unable, on arrival, to meet the attendance requirements for sitting University Entrance, he repeated his fifth form (Year 11) year and, due to constrained family finances, concluded secondary schooling at the end of Year 12. Thereafter Steve worked as a stock controller and trainee accountant, formative experiences that cemented his resolve to work with people rather than numbers, and provided the necessary resources to support his initial teacher education.

As a beginning teacher, Steve identified Wainuiomata as one of his preferred placement areas. He readily confesses that "more of a sense of social life" than social justice inspired his first choice of school, but subsequent moves proved more deliberate in their professional intent. His first principalship was of a decile 10 city school, far removed from the social and political milieu of his youth and early adulthood. In this community Steve enjoyed animated conversations with new acquaintances but soon recognised that cultural and philosophical divides meant he "always seemed to draw back to Wainui for real friendship." Applying to become principal of Te Wharau was thus "a conscious decision … I wasn't really a decile 10 person and I think there are more important places to be than a decile 10 school." Having done his homework, Steve had no qualms about leading a lower decile school in a predominantly Māori community. He feels strong affinity with Māori, something he treasures rather than rationalises, and a number of Wainuiomata connections held him in good stead for the move north:

> A lot of Ngāti Porou live in Wainui … there was a huge movement from Gisborne to Auckland and Wellington … and a lot of them settled in Wainuiomata because it was so cheap at that stage. When [I said] I was going to Gisborne, every single one said, 'Oh, I've got an aunty', 'I've got an uncle', 'Oh my family's from there' … 'Look out for such and such', or 'Go and ring such and such'.

In the event, Steve was so busy "getting the school right" that he had little opportunity to follow contacts up.

Pursuing social justice

Asked to articulate what social justice means, Steve offers the following definition:

> To me, social justice is about equity and giving each child the chance to succeed in life and to be a good citizen. To get the knowledge of what being a good citizen is and also seeing that there's a pathway

away from not being a good citizen. It's making things available for
them to realise that life does not have to be violent … and that there's
a way to get out of the poverty cycle. And also to provide them with
better ways to cope with being poor. Rediscovering themselves.

Steve's conception of social justice is an expansive one that encompasses individual identity and collective citizenry. Individual identity is
about growing culturally secure and resourceful young people who are
comfortable in their own skin and able to cope with and overcome adver-
sity. Collective citizenry not only involves manaakitanga (respectful,
caring relationships with others) but also kaitiakitanga (guardianship
and conservation of the environment). Steve is attuned to the need to
balance competing tensions between individual and collective concepts
of social justice and the leadership dilemma that this creates:

> How long do you keep a child who's interrupting the education of
> twenty other kids and getting in the way of their learning? How long
> do you let that person's rights override the rights of the others? It's a
> tricky decision.

At the outset, he was shocked to discover that while his city school
"decile 10, white, were wanting to come up and hand [him] over,"
Te Wharau was not well placed to extend their new principal a traditional pōwhiri (formal Māori welcome). Steve thus identified the need
to lift Māori language and identity as the biggest challenge facing him
upon arrival. Perceiving cultural location as fundamental to esteem
and self-actualisation, Steve was troubled to discover "a lot that don't
identify. We have a number [of families] who I feel have lost their iwi—
they are just urban Māori with no connection." Efforts to re-establish
cultural connections included forging links with the local marae and
gangs, inviting community elders to teach children about their local
heritage, and marae stays:

> Our Year 4s go and stay on the marae and that is really quite an eye-
> opener. The ones that have done it in the past are fish to water and
> then there's the others that just have no idea and they're scared, some
> of them.

As important as self-actualisation is, Steve understands that meeting children's core physiological needs is a critical prerequisite for
learning. In New Zealand the provision of basic nutrition is deemed a

parental responsibility and, while there has been recent political pressure to do so, the state does not currently provide free or subsidised school lunch programmes for underprivileged children. Recognising that children's ability to focus on learning rests on adequate nutrition, Te Wharau, like many schools, has enlisted community and corporate support to meet these needs. In addition to the breakfast club, which has been operating for 6–7 years, the school belongs to the Anchor *Milk in Schools* scheme and there are scheduled "brain food breaks" during which children consume donated fruit. Teachers surreptitiously ensure that all children have food for lunch and the school provides emergency lunches for those who do not. In a twist on the traditional eat-then-play pattern during lunch breaks, children play first and eat during the final 15 minutes. Steve reports that while this might seem counter-intuitive, children are less likely to gobble food down in their eagerness to run around, or to skip lunch altogether. Teachers consequently find them more settled and focused during afternoon class.

The dignity of children is also protected in the provision of essential learning materials. Steve uses approximately $7,000 of special needs funding to purchase stationery for children at the beginning of the school year. This ensures that learning time is maximised, that poor children are not easily identified, and that stationery is of a reasonable quality:

> So many of our kids don't look at books or write or read during the
> Christmas break, so we have our teachers work right up to the last
> day and then we start on the first day because they've got all their
> stationery … the idea is the teachers start right off the bat, they start
> running on the first day.

While the school provides basic food and equipment, Steve firmly believes in a hand up over a hand out. Te Wharau has an extensive environmental programme that includes conservation of the endangered kaka beak plant and "probably the biggest school gardens in the country." Twenty fruit trees are almost at the point of providing. All children grow a range of produce that they harvest and use, in the process gaining horticultural, environmental, and food technology knowledge and skills. Parents are given surplus produce and pressure from children to grow vegetables at home has drawn many into the school to find out more about gardening. Entrepreneurial activities include the production and sale of a recipe book, and firebricks made from recycled paper. Financial literacy is another priority: "One of our poorest families last year, the kid had twenty dollars virtually every day to buy their lunch. This is where I believe in teaching them about how to spend money."

Safety and a sense of belonging

When Steve arrived at Te Wharau, there were a number of students with learning and behavioural difficulties. The changing nature of the student intake had meant that some teachers struggled to accommodate children's needs and Steve identified this as a pressing concern:

> When I first arrived, there were teachers who were still thinking it was more a decile 4 or 5 than a decile 1. When I arrived, it was decile 3 and then a 2 and then a 1—bang, bang, bang—but there were a number of teachers who didn't cope with that change and couldn't understand the poverty, couldn't understand the life that these kids were going home to.

Complicating matters was a tendency for teachers to send disruptive children to the deputy principal and the latter's conviction that absolving teachers from disciplinary responsibilities enabled them to get on with the job of teaching. To the contrary, Steve argued, "If they were constantly just saying, 'you've misbehaved, get out of my classroom', they weren't teaching the kids behaviour that was expected."

When, in 2006, a senior teacher alerted Steve to the disjunction between teachers imploring children to use their manners and 5-year-olds having even a basic understanding of the concept, the school initiated their own values programme, CHARM. An acronym for the desired values of co-operation, honesty, attitude, resilience, and manners, CHARM guides learning and behaviour expectations that apply equally to students and staff. In addition to dedicated, co-constructed values lessons, CHARM now includes circle time, an initiative that aligns well with Māori hui and group learning processes, and provides students with the language and opportunity to voice their feelings, to resolve conflict, to generate possible solutions, and to reach consensus. Incidents of bullying are now infrequent and typically low-level.

Students are allowed to play bullrush and rugby, with the understanding that they police these games themselves, and Steve is contemplating introducing a student judicial panel that will decide the outcome for students involved in foul play. Behaviour has improved to the point that:

> Most people come in and find it hard to believe that we're decile 1. And when they walk through the classes, you know, the kids are on-task and learning … we've just had our ERO visit and one of our ERO people was Māori … and she couldn't get over the way our kids walked tall, walked proud; that they weren't slouching and scuffing their feet; they had smiles on their face; they said hello, they were friendly—which is all part of the CHARM programme, being charming.

The school has worked hard to make whānau feel welcome and supported caregivers to become more proactive towards their children's schooling. In addition to visiting homes, the school regularly invites parents to sporting and performance events, makes computers available for parents to use, and provides a sausage sizzle on report evenings. Steve believes that these and other initiatives have strengthened home–school partnerships, to the extent that attendance at report evenings has risen from under 50% to approximately 80%. The vibrant school website is regularly maintained and Steve uses school newsletters to take a moral stand on a range of issues. In one December pānui (newsletter), he discouraged parents from buying expensive smart phones, iPads, and gaming consoles as Christmas presents and, in another, recommended a range of low-cost holiday activities that combine family fun and learning. Recognising and endeavouring to ease the financial burden on parents is yet another example of concern for community.

The concept of manaakitanga also extends to staff. The senior team "go out of our way to make sure that our teachers don't burn out." This includes restricting meeting frequency and duration, providing impromptu refreshments when they sense morale and energy levels are low, allowing staff two discretionary leave days per year (with the proviso that no school work be undertaken during this time), and keeping paperwork to a bare minimum. Steve is alert to external accountabilities that divert staff from their core work and seeks to protect them from these:

Most of my job is to do all the bureaucratic stuff and keep my teachers
focused on teaching and learning. I do a lot of mundane Ministry
stuff so they don't have to. I took on Novopay issues ... targets, and
reporting on targets ... I do all that to free [teachers] up to work with
their kids and to be with their kids ... we make it so that they can
channel all their energy towards improving their kids' learning, rather
than sending out huge amounts of assessment data to us.

Steve recognises that dedicated and skilled staff are critical. He
argues furthermore that low-decile schools require a different skillset
than high-decile schools:

I do believe that the teachers who teach here have more all-round
skills than teachers in decile 10. I do believe that there's a special
quality of teacher for a decile 10 and there's a different quality for a
teacher of a decile 1 ... they [decile 10 teachers] don't have behaviour
issues, they don't have to change the kid, the kid is already focused
on education and it's leading him in the right direction; whereas here,
we're trying to find the direction for them as well.

As previously noted, the changing nature of the student intake presented teachers with relational and pedagogical challenges that many
were unaccustomed to. Confronting existing teacher attitudes and introducing culturally responsive pedagogy was an essential but frustratingly
slow undertaking, which required considerable resolve on Steve's part:

It was [a] case of trying to get them to change or move on, and that
took a number of years ... It was getting staff to take ownership of
the problem because, in the past, they had been sending disruptive
students to the DP, and what they were losing was their own agency.

Steve's resolute approach to maintaining quality teaching is consistent with his social justice philosophy. In addition to high performance
expectations, the use of recruitment and appointment processes
accelerated cultural change and, unlike other low-decile schools that
struggle to attract and retain suitably qualified staff, Te Wharau now
fields "huge amounts of applications ... there's a lot of teachers who
would like to get here." Staff turnover is low; a number have taught
at the school for over 10 years, and three are former students. Many
staff live within the local community and those who do not "still have
connections to the community or some sort of affinity towards the

community." Deep connection with community means that staff "are not wanting to rest on laurels … are wanting to develop" and Steve readily attributes school success to their commitment and innovation.

Staying ALIVE

The acronym ALIVE (Active, Limitless/liberated/learning/lifelong, Involved/invigorating, Vibrant and Engaging/energetic) encapsulates the learning environment that the school aspires to create. Informed by *Ka Hikitia* (Ministry of Education, 2013), the school curriculum prioritises student engagement. An experiential focus sees "Freaky Fantastic Funky Fridays or Weird Wonderful Wacky Wednesdays" where children:

> might spend a whole day doing something outside the classroom, or doing something outside regular lessons that are based around things that either [teachers] know will interest the kids, or based around the kids' interests. And then they base their writing, take it back into the classroom and work on it from that point on … the ALIVE School is very much trying to take advantage of those teaching moments.

Wary of the potential for a rigid focus on literacy and numeracy to stultify learning, Steve is determined to ensure that these "teaching moments [don't] start disappearing."

He believes scanning the educational environment for targeted learning initiatives is another core leadership responsibility. Selected literacy innovations, for example, include oral language (HPP—Hei ahiahi ki te panui pukapuka) and reading skill development (PPP—pause, prompt, praise), First Chance, AVAILLL (Audio Visual Achievement in Literacy, Language and Learning), and Clicker6. Both deputy principals are walking DPs,[2] which gives them the flexibility to personalise the learning of smaller groups of children, in class and out of class. In Steve's view this enhances equity of learning provision. In a similar vein, weekly units of work run from Wednesday to Wednesday, rather than Monday to Friday "because our absences are often Monday and Friday so, by changing that around, the kids are here for the beginning and end."

---

2   A walking DP works with teachers in multiple classes, rather than having a single class permanently assigned to them.

Student progress is regularly monitored without being constantly measured against prescribed standards. Because the high level of transience masks overall achievement, Steve disaggregates school data to distinguish the attainment of children for whom Te Wharau is their only school and those who have attended multiple schools. Not only are children achieving above the national standard in literacy and numeracy, they also outperform students in other low-decile schools. While he supports the need for literacy and numeracy standards in principle, Steve finds narrow measures of learning, relentless target setting, and inter-school comparisons futile:

> Much as I dislike National Standards, and I think it's going to
> actually harm our kids more than help them, we do achieve pretty
> good results compared to national. But that's just more of a look-in
> for ourselves, rather than to start blabbing about the neighbourhood
> with it. It's the follow up that's a worry, it's the next steps where they
> start comparing schools … We set targets and I had them up in the
> staffroom so teachers were constantly aware of them. One of them
> said, 'How can we be ALIVE when you keep putting that up?' So the
> targets disappeared real quick! And, as a staff, we don't say 'targets'
> because we work towards the individual, we really believe in the
> individual … we don't say that we've got five Māori boys who need
> to be lifted up and our target is to do x, which is what the Ministry
> is pushing. We look at the kids and say, okay, these kids are falling
> behind, what can we do for these kids? … We don't say we want them
> to be at such and such a level; we want them to get as far ahead as
> they possibly can.

Contesting injustice

Contesting injustice includes challenging the Ministry of Education over target setting and the adoption of enrolment schemes that include children from wealthier residential areas and exclude children from poorer ones. Steve perceives that unethical zoning intensifies residential segregation. When a large primary school in the city proposed a school zone that avoided "a really poor state housing area … closer than the predominantly white area that they included," he argued that the Ministry was perpetuating social injustice: "I believe the more that they encourage or allow white flight to happen, the more it separates us as a nation." Census data (Statistics New Zealand, 2013) for Outer Kaiti (in which approximately 30% of residents identify as Pākeha, 78% as Māori, and 10% as Pasifika)[3] and the adjacent Wainui area (89% Pākeha, 18% Māori, 1% Pasifika) support his view that the city's population is highly stratified.

Reflections for readers

As noted elsewhere (Morrison, McNae, & Branson, 2015), social justice is a fluid and contested notion. In the absence of a nationally accepted definition of, and commitment to, social justice, New Zealand school leaders and their communities must decipher for themselves what social justice means and what the pursuit of socially just outcomes involves. People hold multiple views as to what constitutes a social justice leader and who determines this: "That the same term is used by both the political right and political left to mean quite different things attests to the problematic nature of social justice" (Angelle, Morrison, & Stevenson, 2015, pp. 98–99). Within this diversity, however, ISLDN network members commonly agree that social justice leaders relentlessly pursue greater equity in educational access, opportunity, and outcome. While it is true that leadership endeavours occur at multiple levels within schools and transcend positional roles, the ultimate responsibility for building internal school culture and mediating external policy directives rests with school principals. This makes their explicit commitment to principles of social justice crucial in cultivating an inclusive learning environment that openly confronts injustice and reconciles the conflicts arising from competing forms of, and claims to, social justice.

Steve's example suggests that social justice leaders also seek out school contexts in which they believe they can most fully exercise agency. As principal, Steve is constantly "looking for ways that I feel will improve the school; that will improve our learning outcomes." His leadership for social justice is embedded in daily and often instinctive actions that take multiple forms and operate on multiple fronts. Knowing that students' life chances depend on their formative schooling lends urgency to his work and it is the doing, rather than the theorising, that matters most.

---

3   Census data include people who identify with more than one ethnicity. As a result, percentages do not add up to 100.

In the doing, however, Steve's leadership exemplifies Maslow's (1943) hierarchy of needs and the three forms of justice expounded by Gewirtz and Cribb (2002): distributive, associational, and cultural. Distributive justice draws on Rawlsian notions of social justice (Rawls, 1972) and focuses primarily on the allocation of material resources, but may also include other forms of social and cultural capital (Bourdieu, 1977). In this instance, a commitment to distributive justice involves allocating resources such as food, stationery, and one-on-one teacher time in ways that reflect need, something that sits comfortably with most educators. Less common in schools is sustained attention to associational and cultural dimensions of justice. Associational justice focuses on power and the ability of different individuals and groups to participate in decision-making processes, while cultural justice is concerned with the extent to which different cultural groups are valued and recognised. This involves a commitment to inclusion, and to challenging injustices that arise from both institutionalised and individualised racism, including epistemic and symbolic violence (Bourdieu, 1991) that arises when the curriculum privileges certain forms of knowing over others. Creating space for children to share their voice in classroom circle time and empowering them to adjudicate infringements on the playing field; ensuring that the school curriculum remains ALIVE; aligning curriculum delivery to attendance patterns whilst simultaneously collaborating in multi-agency interventions to change these patterns; and advocating publicly for equitable enrolment zones all serve to illustrate Steve's commitment to associational and cultural justice.

Cribb and Gewirtz's (2005) analysis highlights the challenge and complexity in pursuing social justice. The distribution, and redistribution of resources, in their varied forms, is necessarily a political act in which the status quo must be continually questioned. Not only does this demand the courage to speak out, the resilience to persevere in the face of both open and veiled resistance, and the willingness to "embrace complexity and live with ambivalences" (Cribb & Gewirtz, 2005, p. 338), it requires hope (Bernardo, 2010; Snyder, 2002) and eternal optimism. Knowing that some affluent Pākehā parents choose to enrol their children in schools that give them a "chance to be part of Gisborne, rather than part of a half of Gisborne" is heartening. Steve is similarly confident that schools like Te Wharau "are going to be the ones that break that boundary and that barrier down. The more we can instil in our kids, the better it's going to be for everyone in Gisborne."

Questions to ponder

- To what extent does your personal definition of social justice resonate with Steve's and with the literature?

- What life and career events have heightened your awareness of injustice?

- How do you disrupt unjust practices in your educational setting?

- In what ways do you respect and enhance associational and cultural justice?

- What enables, constrains, and sustains your pursuit of greater equity in educational access, opportunity, and outcome?

- What personal and professional insights does Steve's leadership story offer you?

References

Angelle, P., Morrison, M., & Stevenson, H. (2015). "Doing" social justice leadership: Connecting the macro and micro contexts of schooling. In D. Armstrong & J. Ryan (Eds.), *Working (with/out) the system: Educational leadership, micropolitics and social justice* (pp. 95–117). Charlotte, NC: Information Age Publishing.

Bernardo, A. B. I. (2010). Extending hope theory: Internal and external locus of hope. *Personality and individual differences, 49*(8), 944–949. doi 10.1016/j.paid.2010.07.036

Bourdieu, P. (1991). *Language and symbolic power.* Cambridge, MA: Harvard University Press.

Bourdieu, P. (1997). The forms of capital. In A. H. Halsey, H. Lauder, P. Brown, & A. Stuart Wells (Eds.), *Education: Culture, economy, society* (pp. 46–58). Oxford, UK: Oxford University Press.

Bull, C. (2011). *Gisborne/East Coast District community profile: For the Community Response Model Forum.* Wellington: Ministry of Social Development. Retrieved from www.gdc.govt.nz/assets/CommitteeMeetings/11-493-1X-Appendix.pdf

Cribb, A., & Gewirtz, S. (2005). Navigating justice in practice: An exercise in grounding ethical theory. *Theory and Research in Education, 3*(3), 327–342.

Gewirtz, S., & Cribb, A. (2002). Plural conceptions of social justice:
Implications for policy sociology. *Journal of Education Policy, 17*(5), 499–
509. doi: 10.1080/02680930210158285

Maslow, A. H. (1943). A theory of human motivation. *Psychological Review,
50(4),* 370–396.

Ministry of Education. (2013). *Ka Hikitia—Accelerating success 2013–2017:
The Māori education strategy.* Wellington: Author.

Ministry of Social Development. (2013). *Gisborne Youth Action Plan July
2013—June 2015.* Wellington: Author. Retrieved from http://www.msd.
govt.nz/documents/about-msd-and-our-work/work-programmes/initiatives/
social-sector-trials/gisborne-action-plan-dec-2013.pdf

Morrison, M., McNae, R., & Branson, C. M. (2015). Multiple hues: New
Zealand school leaders' perceptions of social justice. *Journal of Educational
Leadership, Policy and Practice, 30*(1), 4–16.

Rawls, J. (1971). *A theory of justice.* Cambridge, MA: Harvard University Press.

Snyder, C. R. (2002). Hope theory: Rainbows in the mind. *Psychological
Inquiry, 13*(4), 249–275.

Statistics New Zealand. (2013). *2013 Census: Profile and summary reports.*
Wellington: Author. Retrieved from http://www.stats.govt.nz/Census/2013-
census/profile-and-summary-reports.aspx

Chapter 7 **In search of equity and excellence: A story of leadership from a rural school community**

Mere Berryman and Zac Anderson

Introduction

As in many other colonised countries, education in Aotearoa New Zealand continues to perpetuate a situation where disproportionate numbers of indigenous Māori students remain marginalised from the full benefits of education. For Māori students to take their rightful place as successful and valuable contributors to society, education as it is currently constituted must be transformatively reimagined and reformed. This requires school leaders who understand the need to be guided by the Māori communities in which they are located, as they build relationships of respect and trust and engage in a culturally responsive manner. This chapter follows members of a rural community and college on their journey into and through Te Kotahitanga (Unity of Purpose), a secondary school reform initiative.

Te Wairoa Hōpūpū Hōnengenenge Mātangi Rau: The river and its town

The principal, school, and community central to this chapter are all located in Wairoa (long water), a small Hawke's Bay township nestled

alongside the Wairoa River, on the east coast of the North Island. The
population of Wairoa District in 2013 was 7,890, 59% of whom identified as Māori (Wairoa District Council, 2016a). The major iwi and hapū
(tribes and sub-tribes) represented in Wairoa are Ngāti Kahungunu ki
Te Wairoa (45%), along with Tūhoe (15%), Ngāti Porou (13%), and
Rongomaiwahine Te Mahia (12%) (Statistics New Zealand, 2016).
Wairoa District supports the region's main industries of agriculture,
forestry, fishing, and manufacturing. Almost halfway between Napier
and Gisborne on State Highway 2, Wairoa District encompasses six
regions: Mahia, Maungataniwha–Tuai, Nuhaka–Whakaki, Raupunga,
Ruakituri–Morere, and Frasertown.

Originally a Māori settlement from the ancestral canoe Tākitumu,
Wairoa is home to 37 marae (cultural spaces). A fundamental source
of food for the community, the river's traditional name—Te Wairoa
Hōpūpū Hōnengenenge Mātangi Rau—translates as "the long, bub-
bling, swirling, uneven waters" (Wairoa District Council, 2016b,
p. 2). The Wairoa District Council embraces the following whakataukī
(cultural saying) for their region: Hapori Tūhono. Āhua Noho Tōrere.
Taiao Piki Kōtuku (Connected Communities. Desirable Lifestyles.
Treasured Environments).

Despite these 'desirable lifestyles and treasured environments',
Wairoa is a community that has often struggled to rise above the negative images portrayed in the media of poverty, unemployment, rival
gangs, domestic abuse, and crime. As with many small towns throughout Aotearoa constrained by isolation, Wairoa continues to deal with
population decline and the vulnerabilities of economic downturn. That
being said, the residents of Wairoa work hard to promote the economic,
social, environmental, and cultural wellbeing of their community.

Wairoa College is the only secondary school in the district and
serves students from Years 7 to 13. In 2009, Wairoa College was a
decile 1 school educating 505 students, of whom 87% identified as
Māori. It was at this time that the Māori community began to openly
express their concerns about the educational success of their tamariki
mokopuna (children and grandchildren). This is the story of the benefits
that accrued when, with the support of the community, the principal of Wairoa College proposed they should join Te Kotahitanga. By
exploring the journey of how the Wairoa community engaged with Te

Kotahitanga from the end of 2009 to the beginning of 2013, we seek to build a picture of the culturally responsive and relational knowledge, skills, and dispositions they developed to ensure more equitable outcomes for their Māori learners. This chapter outlines how, by working collaboratively, leadership for educational reform was demonstrated through a tenacious desire to engage in professional learning and school reform that would ultimately begin to change the very fabric of the community in which they lived.

Te Kotahitanga, 2001–13

Te Kotahitanga was developed as an iterative professional development and research project aimed at improving the educational achievement of indigenous Māori students in mainstream New Zealand secondary school classrooms (Bishop, Berryman, Cavanagh, & Teddy, 2007). Te Kotahitanga embraced the self-determination of Māori students by gathering narratives of experience from engaged and non-engaged Māori students across five English-medium secondary schools, along with their whānau (extended family), teachers, and principals (Bishop & Berryman, 2006). Students highlighted the fundamental impact that positive and agentic relationships and interactions with their teachers had on their learning, which led to the development of the Te Kotahitanga Effective Teaching Profile and the associated Culturally Responsive Pedagogy of Relations (Bishop et al., 2007).

The Effective Teaching Profile listed what these Māori students said would engage them in education. It was proposed that by following this profile, teachers could operationalise a culturally responsive and relational pedagogy in their practice (Bishop et al., 2007). Subsequently, the Te Kotahitanga professional development team facilitated learning opportunities for schools to engage with the Effective Teaching Profile in order to create learning contexts:

> where power is shared between self-determining individuals within non-dominating relations of interdependence; where culture counts; where learning is interactive, dialogic and spirals; where participants are connected to one another through the establishment of a common vision for what constitutes excellence in educational outcomes.
> (Bishop et al., 2007, p. 1)

Phase 1 of Te Kotahitanga commenced in 2001, with a small team of researchers introducing professional development to individual teachers in a range of classrooms, to explore how changes in classroom relationships and interactions impacted on improving the outcomes of Māori learners. Phase 2 of Te Kotahitanga (2002–03) was implemented with researchers and a newly developed in-school facilitation model. This phase provided further in-class support to three new schools. Phase 3 of Te Kotahitanga began in 2004 and expanded to work with over 400 teachers in 12 secondary schools. The in-school professional learning of facilitators was supported by the Research and (Professional) Development team and focused on the implementation of the Effective Teaching Profile in classrooms, supported by their principals and an in-school facilitation team. As the project grew, an additional 21 schools were added in 2007 for Phase 4 and regional co-ordinators were employed to provide professional development with the in-school facilitation teams supported by the Research and Development team.

Phase 5 began at the end of 2009 when a further 16 schools, with a mean decile of 3, were introduced to the project. As the Ministry of Education's parameters broadened to include the Central North region, Phase 5 presented the first opportunity for schools on the East Coast of the North Island to be involved in the project. Phase 5 was informed by earlier phases and incorporated "new knowledge around leadership, school–whānau connections, implementation, scaling up, autonomy, accountability, momentum, and sustainability" (Alton-Lee, 2015, p. 7). It was at this stage of the development of Te Kotahitanga that Wairoa College joined this professional learning reform initiative.

Wairoa College's Te Kotahitanga journey

The community

At the beginning of 2009, members of the Wairoa Māori community, all mothers and grandmothers, approached the team at the University of Waikato, expressing their concerns about the lack of educational success of their tamariki mokopuna. This all-female contingent had heard about the successes of Te Kotahitanga from whānau members in other parts of the country. They asked the question of the Waikato team, "How can we have Te Kotahitanga at Wairoa College?" As mana whenua (customary authority exercised by an iwi or hapū), these women openly and honestly expressed their desire to engage in Te Kotahitanga as a way of improving future life chances for their tamariki mokopuna. In supporting their own whakapapa (bloodline), they understood that this would benefit their turangawaewae (the place upon which they stand) and their community. Wairoa College was placed on the Te Kotahitanga list for inclusion should the Ministry approve Phase 5. The vision of this group and the voices of others on the list became important talking points in the discussions for a new phase.

The principal

Towards the end of 2009, members of the Te Kotahitanga team talked with the principal of Wairoa College about his application to participate in Te Kotahitanga. The teaching career of this principal had spanned 38 years, with the last 10 years as a principal. He identified that improving Māori student outcomes was a top priority for him, his staff, and, in particular, for the Māori community the college served. The principal openly recognised the challenges in shifting teachers' pedagogy from a largely top-down transmission model to one that was more dialogic and engaging with the students' own cultural toolkits (Bruner, 1996). The principal acknowledged that these changes would be essential. Speaking with a member of the Te Kotahitanga team, the principal recounted how he had learnt this lesson himself. As a young and relatively new teacher in a predominantly Māori rural secondary school, many of his early lessons were spent with his back to the class while he wrote copious notes on the board. He recalls the advice of a young Māori boy who was confident enough to share with him that if teachers were to let students share ideas and talk about their work, they would learn more together. He commented that this experience had been one of those 'aha!' moments that he had never forgotten. This was perhaps the beginning of his conscious awareness of how to work more effectively with students, especially those he had previously found difficult to engage with.

First, he had to create relational contexts, where students were comfortable to say what they thought, where he was prepared to hear what his students were saying, and then be courageous enough to try out what they were suggesting. This was the beginning of his understanding about culturally responsive and relational pedagogy, terms that were not used at the time. Nor was this pedagogy common in the classrooms of his colleagues. This experience, and his engagement with Te Kotahitanga, continued to inform his leadership practice and his understanding of the fundamental importance of engaging in relationships of connectedness with students, staff, and the community as a means by which to listen and take advice. The top-down transactional leader was beginning to illustrate practices associated with equity and social justice for the students and community he was seeking to serve.

During the early stages of their Te Kotahitanga journey, the principal was able to articulate the complex challenges he and his community would encounter. This included addressing deficit theorising from staff, fostering environments in classrooms where Māori students could bring their language, identity, and culture to their learning, and, in particular, deprivatising teacher practice. The latter would enable effective observations and feedback sessions followed by the sharing of evidence to show what was really happening for Māori students in their classrooms. An important early stage of their engagement with Te Kotahitanga was their first Hui Whakarewa (to set in motion) held on a local marae. Hui Whakarewa involve the school-based facilitation team, having engaged in prior learning with the Te Kotahitanga team, introducing and launching Te Kotahitanga with staff and, on the final evening, members of the Māori community. The principal noted one of the highlights of the hui was the positive extent to which staff participated in sharing their stories and learning about their own and others' positioning around how they engage their Māori learners. The feedback he received from the community was genuine and heartwarming, and he acknowledged the school had taken a big step forward with the community.

Becoming a Te Kotahitanga school

From the outset, the leadership team at Wairoa College openly expressed their intent: "We are a Te Kotahitanga school." This statement was shared widely on the school website, in conversations with the community and the student body, and when advertising for new staff members. Te Kotahitanga was unique in its unwavering concern with improving the educational outcomes for Māori students in mainstream secondary schools in Aotearoa. Phase 5 schools engaged with tools and learning that supported a relentless focus on accelerating educational reform. In a demonstration report on the effectiveness of Phase 5 of Te Kotahitanga, Alton-Lee (2015) showed that Te Kotahitanga did indeed accomplish accelerated outcome trajectories for Māori students, despite Organisation for Economic Co-operation and Development (OECD) reports that the secondary education system in New Zealand was experiencing a period of accelerated decline. For Phase 5 schools, the achievement rate for Māori students across National Certificate of Educational Achievement (NCEA) Levels 1–3 by 2012 had improved by three times the rate of Māori students in non-Te Kotahitanga schools (Alton-Lee, 2015).

When evaluating the effectiveness of Te Kotahitanga in addressing the aspirations of *Ka Hikitia* (Ministry of Education, 2103), Alton-Lee (2015) acknowledged that, "it is only through deep-seated cultural and pedagogical change that a teacher, leader, institution or system can enable substantive change for Māori" (p. 8). Alton-Lee (2015) used a Best Evidence Synthesis perspective to identify seven critical factors for success as levers for educational improvement. These factors centre on the importance of indigenous educational expertise, whakawhanau-ngatanga (establishing relationships), effective teaching and professional development, transformative leadership, educationally powerful connections, and collaborative research and development cycles.

The Wairoa educational community acknowledged that, to be transformative, the knowledge and expertise of the Māori community must be validated, honoured, and embraced. In this way, Māori students and their extended whānau remained at the heart of the mahi (work). By engaging with kaumātua and kuia (Māori elders), Wairoa College demonstrated an understanding that Māori educational expertise would lead to a culturally responsive approach to accelerating the outcomes for their Māori learners.

Whakawhanaungatanga is a concept embedded in te ao Māori (the Māori world) and enables participants to advance a kaupapa (shared vision) by building relationships of respect and trust. Engaging in whakawhanaungatanga from the outset enabled college staff to address how issues of power played out in interactions. When power was shared, within a reciprocal relationship of care and connectedness, cultural repositioning paved the way for the development of manaaki-tanga (belief in and care for Māori learners), mana motuhake (high expectations for Māori learners and their learning), and mahi tahi (to do the work as one) with moral purpose and accountability (Alton-Lee, 2015). Whakawhanaungatanga became evident across the key elements of Wairoa's participation in Te Kotahitanga as well as being the essential building block for teachers wishing to implement the Effective Teaching Profile. Whakawhanaungatanga served as a vehicle for building relational trust and culturally responsive relationships during every stage of the professional development with teachers and leaders. A Year 12 student expressed their feelings about the importance of solid relationships: "Awesome year! We are able to awhi [surround and embrace] each other."

Engaging with the Effective Teaching Profile enabled teachers and leaders at the college to focus on implementing a culturally responsive and relational pedagogy that optimised the classroom as a community of learners. Teachers engaged in classroom practices that demonstrated a shift in practice from a traditional model of transmission of knowledge to a more dialogic and interactive model. Teachers successfully implementing the Effective Teaching Profile demonstrated ako (teachers and learners embracing reciprocal approaches). Within ako, teachers and learners embrace the understanding that knowledge is never fixed, but spirals and builds on previous knowledge to co-construct new knowledge.

This approach to embedding culturally responsive and relational pedagogies was also reflected in the professional development of teachers. By moving away from the traditional 'expert' model of Professional Learning and Development delivery, the teachers and leaders at Wairoa College engaged in professional learning activities that prioritised evidence-based decision making to inform practice and therefore co-construct new knowledge with the very people they were seeking to support. The Te Kotahitanga team at Wairoa College recognised from the outset that by exposing teachers to cultural dissonance (Bishop & Berryman, 2010) they might understand more deeply the imbalances of power that existed in their classrooms. Teachers and leaders engaged in professional learning that encouraged them to reposition themselves as learners and their Māori students as their teachers (Sleeter, Bishop, &

Meyer, 2011). A Year 13 student who was about to graduate expressed the following:

> Over the years it has improved. Not only in the quality of the work given to us, but also in the way teachers are involving themselves in our learning. There seems to be more effort being put into caring about and helping us in the classroom.

In order to institutionalise deep educational change, the principal, board of trustees, and other senior leaders at Wairoa College played an increasingly active role in "championing, brokering, and sharing stories of improvement" (Alton-Lee, 2015, p. 52) within their community of practice. Participants engaging in co-construction meetings at three levels—classroom, middle leaders, and senior leaders—also embraced transformative educational leadership. These meetings focused on "collaborative problem-solving and direction-setting based on evidence of students/groups of students' educational performance in relation to established goals" (Sleeter et al., 2011, p. 168). Co-construction meetings enabled leaders to assert their agency by engaging in professional learning conversations focused on enacting change for Māori student achievement. One Year 9 student noticed positive outcomes for Māori students, stating: "The amount of Māori students achieving high standards this year is expanding. In every assembly there is a Māori student being called up. I enjoy learning at this school knowing that others can achieve."

The School Leadership and Student Outcomes Best Evidence Synthesis simply states, "making connections is part of good pedagogy" (Robinson, Hohepa, & Lloyd, 2009, p. 169). Interventions that made the most significant impact on educational outcomes were those where parents, whānau, and other community members helped support their children's learning at home, incorporated community and whānau knowledge into the curriculum, alongside teachers developing expertise in their classrooms at the same time. One Year 11 student expressed the importance of sharing their learning journey: "Learning is hard but can be easy with help, so we take our time to make sure it's right."

Teachers and leaders were supported to connect their classroom practice to their learners' identities, whānau, iwi, and local community. As teachers embraced the driving force of the Effective Teaching

Profile, they acquired the humility required to learn from their Māori students and their whānau (Penetito, Hindle, Hynds, Savage, & Kus, 2011). In turn, this increased the likelihood of these teachers embedding culturally responsive pedagogy into their daily practice.

With an unrelenting focus on improving educational outcomes for Māori students, the in-school Te Kotahitanga team at Wairoa College focused on discerning the conditions to maintain, replicate, and sustain the gains they were making (Bishop, Berryman, Wearmouth, Peter, & Clapham, 2011). Teachers developed expertise through a cycle of inquiry, observation, co-construction, and shadow coaching. In this way, teachers at Wairoa College focused on more than academic measures of success. Teachers embraced the importance of locating student learning within their own cultural communities, where te reo Māori (the Māori language), tikanga Māori (customs and traditions), and local culture and history were privileged.

Activating whānau-like relationships

The story of how the Wairoa educational community and their school effectively engaged in improving the educational success of their Māori students as Māori can be illustrated by a number of significant changes and initiatives. Whānau-like relationships within a secondary school community are as varied, dynamic, and flexible as they are in traditional Māori settings. Inherent within the concept of whānau are relationships based on mutual respect and trust. Wairoa College reimagined their learning environments to embrace whānau-like relationships to nurture and support the educational success of Māori students as Māori. The fruits of such nurturing were also exemplified by the new respect students had for their physical space and the relationship formed with the woman who tended the gardens.

Educational leaders at Wairoa College began to use multiple sources of evidence, including AREA (achievement, retention, engagement, and attendance) data. While National Standards, Year 9 and Year 10 achievement data, and NCEA results can paint a picture of educational achievement, they only paint a small portion of the full picture. This prompted the college to delve more deeply into the personal learning journeys of Māori students. They then used this evidence to inform decision making about systems and structures that had traditionally posed barriers to educational success. Teachers with students in common met regularly to share evidence of their pedagogical practice, informed via observation and shadow coaching with a more expert other, to support best practice and to co-construct goals based on a common vision for their Māori learners. Senior students who had chosen a specific vocational pathway engaged with local businesses to promote learning and employment opportunities. The focus became more on the individual learning pathways of students towards NCEA success with key staff, whānau, and the community supporting the initiatives. One such example was the work undertaken with whakairo (traditional Māori carving).

Whakairo

Expertise in whakairo existed both within the school and the community and this knowledge was called upon to create a class for senior Māori boys to learn a craft embedded in te ao Māori. With the support of teachers and community members, the young men engaged in a process of considering their whakapapa and thinking about how to express these connections in their own carvings. They worked through their designs on paper and in kōrero (talking) with whānau, hapū, and iwi and set about the challenge of creating a number of large-scale carving projects. From conception to finished product, the young men had a point of interest they could use for NCEA cross-accreditation. They attained a myriad of credits from the extraordinary evidence provided by their finished carving: English and/or te reo Māori for their oral presentation; visual arts and numeracy via the design process drawings; and media studies from the short film they each created about their learning journey.

The carving school provided a unique context for learning where whānau and community members were welcome to walk through and talk with the young men while they engaged in their mahi. This presented a cultural context for restoring and healing relationships between the community and the college, grounded in te ao Māori. On a visit to the whakairo class, one parent commented that the last time he had been in the college was as a 15-year-old. He recalled how he felt he hadn't belonged at school; whereas sitting alongside his son, he expressed how warm the atmosphere of this classroom was. Two young men expressed their feelings about being involved in whakairo:

"24-hour whakairo was the best thing I have done ever" and "Carving is the best thing that's happened to me, I have had the meanest year ever!"

Services Academy

Another example of promoting whānau-based learning environments, leading to cross-curricula educational achievement, was the creation of a Services Academy. In this context for learning, student time-tables reflected a majority of time spent together in a mixed senior class, aimed at preparing students for acceptance into the armed forces. Alongside their specialist learning areas, students were supported with literacy and numeracy learning by heads of departments. In this way, students were demonstrating self-determination for their own voca-tional pathways and as a whānau, students and teachers supported each other to ensure academic success. Many of the students in the Services Academy actively supported younger students engaging in the CACTUS (Combined Adolescent Challenge Training Unit Support) programme. Engaging the support of local police alongside teachers and members of the community, student participation in CACTUS provided an opportunity to build educationally powerful relationships that promoted perseverance, physical activity, camaraderie, and con-nections between students and adults. A senior student expressed what success felt like for them, saying: "To get the most out of learning you have to put in lots of hard work, but it's worth it."

Te reo

The college also engaged in the teaching and learning of te reo Māori and tikanga Māori. Resourcing full-time teachers of te reo Māori strengthened the total immersion unit in Years 7 and 8. The bilingual unit in Years 9 and 10 was also further supported to ensure students fluent in te reo Māori gained NCEA qualifications. Senior te reo Māori students accessed and achieved tertiary-level papers and scholarship. Community members and te reo Māori teachers joined forces in a cross-iwi engagement to strengthen kapa haka (Māori performing arts) and involvement with Ngā Manu Kōrero (te reo Māori speaking com-petitions), nurturing the talent of Māori students and building on the relationships forged at the primary school level. One Year 9 student said: "I'm learning more than I expected to learn and I kind of like how I am learning."

Sporting and academic achievement

Engaging in high levels of achievement in sport had always been a focus for the college and community. As the relationships between the school and the community developed, the school gates opened more widely for community members to be involved in the coaching and management of sporting teams. The creation of a Rugby Academy, which presented a united front for academic and sporting success, fostered whānau-like learning environments for students who wished to excel in their chosen sport. The boys in the academy, who had often found themselves caught in the discipline system of the college, responded well to the high expectations of the college and community alike and achieved success in sport and academic studies. A Year 11 student expressed their appreciation of the flexibility offered, noting: "They make the timetable suit you so it's more workable."

In consultation with the Māori community, educational leaders introduced a new House-based pastoral system with a vertical whānau class structure across Years 7 to 13. Teachers engaged in academic learning conversations with their students on a daily basis, as well as mentoring and supporting them in a more traditional pastoral sense. A Year 9 student commented: "My learning has increased, I know more and I'm confident about my learning. I participate 100% and encourage others to learn." The new system also promoted competitiveness in academic, sporting, cultural, attendance, and leadership activities. Teachers kept their students from Year 7 until their graduation in Year 13, strengthening the relationships between the school and home. Traditional sports days became more inclusive and accessible for whānau and community members to attend and the competitive nature of these days between the four Houses was enhanced.

Reflections for readers

Critical and kaupapa Māori theories suggest that, by examining issues of privilege and power, we can challenge and disrupt traditional assumptions about equity and justice through an ongoing and spiraling process of conscientisation, resistance, and transformative praxis (Freire, 1972; Smith, 2003). School leaders in Aotearoa who engage in conscientisation openly highlight and become aware of the part they play in maintaining and contributing to the status quo of inequity for

their Māori learners. By asking critical questions such as, "Now that
I have a better understanding of how power and privilege are playing
out, what am I going to do differently?", educationalists engage in resistance to practices that are resulting in inequity. Transformative leaders
can then engage in new liberatory practices that focus on more equitable social realities for Māori learners.

Kaupapa Māori theory emerged from a proactive movement of resistance to the hegemony of colonisation to revitalise Māori language,
culture, and aspirations of self-determination. At its heart, kaupapa
Māori relates to 'being Māori' and is deeply connected to Māori principles and philosophy (Smith, 1992). Kaupapa Māori takes for granted
the legitimacy and validity of the beliefs and practices of Māori, the
Māori language, and the cultural, intellectual, political, and social
legitimacy of Māori people (Smith, 1992). For Māori, the struggle for
autonomy over cultural wellbeing is an essential component of the conscientisation, resistance, and transformative praxis of kaupapa Māori
(Smith, 1997).

Revitalisation and transformation can occur within kaupapa Māori
when the relationships between power and knowledge are openly
addressed. Kaupapa Māori theory compels us to challenge previously
dominant Western ideas of what constitutes valid knowledge and consider counter-narratives to sense making and the generation of new
knowledge. In educational settings, asking critical questions about the
nature of knowledge, how and by whom knowledge is produced, and
for whose benefit, enables leaders to deconstruct hegemonic discourses.
When educational communities deeply consider the counter logic of
kaupapa Māori and critical theories, they are better placed to radically
transform their setting and enable Māori students to enjoy and achieve
educational success as Māori.

The educational leaders in this community could be understood to
be engaging in *critical* leadership. They shifted their thinking in terms
of deficit, marginalisation, oppression, and hegemony, to thinking that
embraced leadership as shared, bi-cultural, equitable, and potential-
focused. By engaging in research-informed professional learning and
development, school leaders developed the *skills* required to implement
what research tells us works for Māori learners. This is "underpinned
by a relentless moral imperative" (Berryman, Eley, Ford, & Egan, 2016,

p. 65), whereby these leaders combined the will and skill to reframe the lived reality of their Māori learners in a responsive, courageous, and urgent manner. As a result, educational reform became more achievable. In order to achieve transformative cultural change in mainstream educational settings in Aotearoa, leadership would do well to embrace critical theory and kaupapa Māori theory (Berryman, Egan, & Ford, 2016). Building upon these theories, two further elements are required—the will and the skill.

Conclusion

It has been important to consider critical and kaupapa Māori theories together with leadership dispositions for educational reform. It has also been important to consider relational and culturally responsive contexts for belonging (Berryman, Nevin, SooHoo, & Ford, 2015). In order to disrupt the status quo of inequity and disenfranchisement of Wairoa's Māori learners, educational leaders and the Māori community engaged in power-sharing relationships as Treaty partners. In the spirit of partnership, they collectively addressed the educational disparities through a process of critical thinking and the use of evidence, to shift practice and better understand issues of power and privilege.

To engage in critical leadership, those who traditionally hold power must "critically examine their own participation and privilege, then seek power-sharing relationships rather than perpetuate the more traditional impositional stance that continues to promote disparities" (Berryman, 2013, p. 9). Wairoa College acknowledged that "it is the less powerful and less privileged who best understand how to transform the relationship" (Berryman, Egan, & Ford, 2016, p. 3). When educational communities reimagine their commitment to using positions of power and privilege for the benefit of all, they can contribute to changing the very fabric of society.

Questions for readers

- In what ways do you critically reflect on sharing power among student, teachers, and community?
- How does kaupapa Māori theory inform your leadership thinking and practice?

References

Alton-Lee, A. (2015). *Ka Hikitia—A demonstration report: Effectiveness of Te
Kotahitanga Phase 5 2010–12*. Wellington: Ministry of Education.

Berryman, M. (2013). Editorial: Culturally responsive pedagogies as
transformative praxis. *Waikato Journal of Education, 18*(2), 3–10.

Berryman, M., Egan, M., & Ford, T. (2016). Examining the potential of
critical and kaupapa Māori approaches to leading education reform in New
Zealand's English-medium secondary schools. *International Journal of
Leadership Education.* doi: 10.1080/13603124.2016.1206973

Berryman, M., Eley, E., Ford, T., & Egan, M. (2016). Leadership: Going
beyond personal will and professional skills to give life to *Ka Hikitia. Journal
of Educational Leadership, Policy and Practice, 30*(2), 56–68.

Berryman, M., Nevin, A., SooHoo, S., & Ford, T. (Eds.). (2015). *Relational
and responsive inclusion: Contexts for becoming and belonging.* New York, NY:
Peter Lang Publishing.

Bishop, R., & Berryman, M. (2006). *Culture speaks: Cultural relationships and
classroom learning.* Wellington: Huia Publishers.

Bishop, R., & Berryman, M. (2010). Te Kotahitanga: Culturally responsive
professional development for teachers. *Teacher Development, 14*(2), 173–187.

Bishop, R., Berryman, M., Cavanagh, T., & Teddy, L. (2007). *Te Kotahitanga
Phase 3 whanaungatanga: Establishing a culturally responsive pedagogy of
relations in mainstream secondary school classrooms.* Wellington: Ministry of
Education.

Bishop, R., Berryman, M., Wearmouth, J., Peter, M., & Clapham, S. (2011).
*A summary of Te Kotahitanga: Maintaining, replicating and sustaining change
in Phase 3 and 4 schools 2007–2010.* Wellington: Ministry of Education.

Bruner, J. (1996). *The culture of education.* Cambridge, MA: Harvard University
Press.

Freire, P. (1972). *Pedagogy of the oppressed.* New York, NY: Continuum.

Ministry of Education. (2013). *Ka Hikitia: Accelerating success 2013–2017.*
Wellington: Author.

Penetito, W., Hindle, R., Hynds, A., Savage, C., & Kus, L. (2011). The impact
of culturally responsive pedagogies on students and families. In C. Sleeter
(Ed.), *Professional development for culturally responsive and relationship-based
pedagogy* (pp. 139–161). New York, NY: Peter Lang Publishing.

Robinson, V., Hohepa, M., & Lloyd, C. (2009). *School leadership and student outcomes: Identifying what works and why. Best Evidence Synthesis Iteration [BES].* Wellington: Ministry of Education.

Sleeter, C., Bishop, R., & Meyer, L. (2011). Professional development for culturally responsive and relationships-based pedagogy. In C. Sleeter (Ed.), *Professional development for culturally responsive and relationship-based pedagogy* (pp. 163–177). New York, NY: Peter Lang Publishing.

Smith, G. H. (1992). *Tane-nui-a-rangi's legacy, propping up the sky: Kaupapa Māori as resistance and intervention.* Paper presented at NZARE/AARE joint conference, Deakin University, Victoria, Australia.

Smith, G. H. (1997). *The development of kaupapa Māori: Theory and praxis.* Unpublished doctoral thesis, The University of Auckland, Auckland.

Smith, G. H. (2003). *Kaupapa Māori theory: Transforming indigenous transformation of education and schooling.* Kaupapa Māori symposium, NZARE/AARE joint conference, Auckland.

Statistics New Zealand. (2016). *2013 Census.* Retrieved from http://nzdotstat.stats.govt.nz/WBOS/Index.aspx?DataSetCode=TABLECODE8053

Wairoa District Council. (2016a). *profile.id: Welcome to the Wairoa District community profile.* Retrieved from http://profile.idnz.co.nz/wairoa/maori

Wairoa District Council. (2016b). *Wairoa River walkway: Historical plaque sites (brochure).* Retrieved from http://www.wairoadc.govt.nz/assets/Document-Library/Publications/River-Walkway/walkwaybrochure.pdf

Chapter 8 When the odds are stacked against: Leadership decisions that shift the odds

Jeanette Clarkin-Phillips

Setting the scene

Involvement in early childhood education has long been regarded as beneficial for children and their families. Ensuring that communities have access to high-quality early childhood education where families feel welcomed can be extremely challenging in the face of reduced funding, particularly in disadvantaged communities. Leadership with a strong sense of social justice is pivotal in providing more equitable opportunities for communities who have the odds stacked against them. Drawing on the findings from a case study of a kindergarten labelled 'vulnerable', the following narrative of the transformation of the kindergarten illustrates the role of leadership in helping shift those odds.

Taitoko Kindergarten, situated in Levin, was opened in the early 1980s under the auspices of the Wellington Region Free Kindergarten Association, now known as He Whānau Manaaki o Tararua[1] Free Kindergarten Association Incorporated. Kindergarten Associations

---

1 Loosely translated to mean 'the caring family of the Tararua region'.

provide services that include central administrative support, leadership, and mentoring by an itinerant 'senior' teacher, professional development opportunities, association-wide policy development, and capital works and maintenance projects.

Initially, Taitoko Kindergarten operated a sessional licence for two groups of 30 children with two teachers. The kindergarten session times (8.45–11.45am and 12.45–2.45pm) mirrored the compulsory school sector calendar. As required by legislation, the kindergarten was staffed by qualified teachers, both of whom held a 2-year New Zealand Kindergarten Diploma. Over the period 2009–12 the kindergarten expanded its hours of operation to align with school hours, and increased the roll to accommodate 42 children including under-2-year-olds. These changes have required an increase in staffing and a major renovation of the environment. There are now 10 teachers employed at the kindergarten.

The kindergarten is located on the 'wrong side of the tracks' in the poorest area of town. The community comprises a range of ethnicities: Māori (41.1%), Pasifika (14.7%), European (63.1%), and Asian (2.0%). In 2004 the fate of the kindergarten hung in the balance due to falling rolls, staffing issues, and a negative reputation: the odds were stacked against it. By 2014 the kindergarten employed 14 staff in various capacities, had expanded its operations, provided a range of services for the community, and offered opportunities for adults to realise their aspirations. The transformation of the kindergarten over a decade is the result of leaders at various levels 'sticking their necks out' to fight the odds.

The first significant event for the kindergarten was the appointment by the Kindergarten Association of a new general manager in 2003. One of the initial decisions faced by Mandy, the new general manager, was about the fate of Taitoko Kindergarten. Two previous general managers had identified Taitoko Kindergarten as a candidate for closure and the current staff seemed to be waiting for the inevitable to happen. However, Mandy convinced the Kindergarten Association board of trustees to keep the kindergarten open. This decision was based on the role that Mandy felt the kindergarten was fulfilling in the community, particularly for young mothers. She chose to take affirmative action in dealing with the issues at the kindergarten, and a well-respected and experienced teacher (Caryll) was appointed in a relieving capacity to work alongside the staff.

Another significant event in the transformation of the kindergarten was its successful bid for a Parent Support and Development (PS&D) contract in 2005. The PS&D was a cross-sectoral early intervention programme for vulnerable children developed by government ministers and officials during 2003–04. Four key elements to the programme included improving health, education, and parent support services for vulnerable children and their families through building on existing universal and targeted services as well as improved co-ordinating, identifying, and needs-assessment by different agencies.

Winning a PS&D contract gave the kindergarten extra funding and enabled the head teacher to be released to build relationships with service agencies in the community so that the teachers could facilitate families' access to support. It also enabled the community to begin to see Taitoko Kindergarten in a more positive light and develop a stronger sense of belonging for families.

Leaders living their values

Prior to her appointment as general manager, Mandy's employment background was in the field of education; first as a primary classroom teacher and then as principal of a primary school in a working class suburb of the city in which she grew up. Her most recent position was as elected head of the country's largest education union. Applying for the position of general manager seemed incongruous with Mandy's beliefs and values about workers and bosses, particularly after her position in the union. However, she was able to reconcile her decision when she realised she had experience and knowledge that could be used in the role and that the values of the kindergarten movement aligned with her own: "That classic belief that our role is actually to make life—to make the world a better place. And that, the role of kindergarten, the role of early childhood education is really to enhance communities."

Rather than act in what would be deemed a fiscally responsible manner and close the kindergarten, Mandy chose to keep it open for the small number of young single mothers ('vulnerable' in the state's eyes) who attended regularly with their children. Mandy's decision implied a commitment to social justice: keeping the kindergarten open, against the odds, to support 'vulnerable' parents. Although the kindergarten continued to face challenges for the next 2 or so years, Mandy saw the benefits that keeping the kindergarten open was having on the community. In the first instance, the kindergarten was providing opportunities for young mothers to feel less socially isolated. As the kindergarten began to build a more positive reputation in the community, it started to become a focal point in the community and closing the kindergarten became a less favourable option. Mandy's commitment to social justice influenced the way in which she viewed the financial viability of kindergartens and how she used resources and regulatory structures to engage in systemic change. Rather than defining a kindergarten's success by its financial health, Mandy used the impact on children and families as the determinant for viability, and looked for other ways to support the financial resourcing of the kindergarten.

Mandy also had a strong belief in empowering others. She demonstrated trust in others' abilities to make decisions for their communities. When Caryll, the new head teacher at Taitoko, saw the advertisement for the PS&D pilot and approached Mandy about applying for a contract, Mandy mobilised personnel and resources within the Kindergarten Association to support the writing of the application. Over the ensuing years of the PS&D contract and beyond, Mandy continued to support the teaching team to implement initiatives at Taitoko Kindergarten.

Empowering others and operating from a strengths-based approach has been integral to the continued success of Taitoko Kindergarten. Caryll was initially asked to relieve and support the teaching team while some of the staffing issues were resolved. She came to Taitoko Kindergarten as an 'outsider', who quickly learned of the reputation of the community. Caryll made a decision to apply for a permanent position at Taitoko Kindergarten based on a mother's negative comments about no one ever staying long at Taitoko. When Caryll told the mother she was staying, the mother queried her decision. Caryll informed her that she felt strongly about families feeling positive about their communities and the opportunities available to their children. Caryll's belief in the right of every child to have a fair and equal chance and her strengths-based acceptance of people led her to ignore and even disrupt the label of 'vulnerable'. She determined very quickly that a priority for the teaching team was to settle on a shared philosophy, which included an acceptance of people "however they come" and that they would be made to feel welcomed. Acceptance and hospitality became significant hallmarks of practice at Taitoko Kindergarten.

The philosophy of empowerment and building leadership capacity has been a significant strength of the kindergarten. In 2012 Caryll accepted Mandy's proposal that Caryll lead the team at another local kindergarten in adapting their centre to be a Pasifika-focused kindergarten. Time frame imperatives meant that Caryll essentially left Taitoko Kindergarten overnight and Tania, a teacher at Taitoko Kindergarten, took over as head teacher. Tania had the confidence to be the head teacher due to Caryll's mentoring and nurturing, coupled with an expectation that she had the skills and qualities to fulfil the role. Tania has continued to build the leadership capacity of parents at the kindergarten as well as empower her colleagues to utilise their strengths in leadership roles.

Shared decision making

As the PS&D contract unfolded, Caryll determined to use the skills and strengths of the community, encouraging them to share the decision making and determine what might work for them. This generated a number of initiatives, which strengthened the place of Taitoko Kindergarten in the community and enhanced the kindergarten's reputation. One of the most successful and sustainable initiatives was a coffee/play group. This was instigated at the suggestion of one of the mothers, Carmella, who Caryll had supported to take on an administrative role at the kindergarten. The administrative role offered Carmella part-time, flexible employment and opportunities to be the 'ear' of the community, which enabled the teaching team to build responsive and reciprocal relationships with families. Carmella felt a coffee/play group would offer informal opportunities for families to come and socialise at the kindergarten, particularly those with younger children who were not attending kindergarten.

The coffee/play group is still operating over a decade later. Parents are responsible for deciding what happens on a weekly basis, with the teachers supporting the organisation and operation of the group. The activities of the coffee/play group range from workshops and guest speakers offering information and practical sessions about a variety of health topics, literacy, child development and parenting, financial literacy, cooking and sewing, and obtaining a driver's licence. These sessions have enabled families to become familiar with different agencies and services and to have a name and a face to connect with if needed. Similarly, the personnel from various agencies have realised the value of building relationships with the kindergarten and being a 'familiar face', breaking down some barriers and misconceptions that were apparent in the community.

Parents' involvement with the coffee/play group has enabled teachers to find out about their strengths and interests and how these might be utilised in the kindergarten programme. The group has also provided an avenue for parents to discuss their aspirations for themselves and their children, and how the kindergarten teachers and management might support these aspirations. Significant changes to the operation of the kindergarten have resulted from these discussions and open consultation. Extended hours of operation to enable children to be at kindergarten for a 'school day' and the provision of affordable, healthy lunches were implemented in 2010. A parent who had previous experience as a chef suggested that the kindergarten provide lunches. This idea was taken up and the parent was employed as the cook. The knowledge that their child could have a substantial lunch regardless of their ability to pay at the time, or at all, helped alleviate the precarious financial situations of a number of the families in the community.

In 2009, despite strong lobbying to a newly elected government, funding for the PS&D ceased. Mandy and her management team were able to continue to fund some of the initiatives such as the kaimahi (cultural support worker) and head teacher release. Their continuation has, however, become increasingly challenging due to persistent funding cuts to the sector. It is the commitment to, and a belief in the benefits for, the community that make resourcing these initiatives a priority for the management.

Families as leaders

The commitment by leaders at both levels of management (Kindergarten Association and head teacher) to build leadership capacity and empower individuals has had far-reaching consequences for the kindergarten community. In a community such as Taitoko, families often lack the social and cultural capital to navigate the machinations of bureaucracy and legislation in order to realise their aspirations. Having someone recognise and support their strengths is empowering. Another key aspect of families sustaining their involvement and developing leadership capabilities has been the non-judgemental, non-stigmatising attitude of the teachers. It was crucial for families that teachers did not make judgements about their parenting skills and life circumstances; families were welcomed unconditionally. For a number of families, being involved in the life of the kindergarten has been life changing.

One of these people is Kirstie. Kirstie grew up in Levin in a single parent family affected by a gambling addiction, and by default she became the major caregiver for her younger sister. Following the death of her mother, 15-year-old Kirstie left school and found employment wherever she could, usually in low-paid, unskilled jobs in fast food outlets. She had her first child when she was 21 who she parented on her own for about 3 years. Kirstie's involvement at Taitoko Kindergarten began when Caryll stopped her on the street one day and suggested she bring her children to kindergarten. Kirstie took up Caryll's invitation:

> I just became part of the kindergarten, literally. When I would go
> in the mornings to drop my kids off, I wouldn't go home. I just
> stayed there and I just hung out, kind of learnt things [about being
> a parent], met people, and was just supported by Caryll. Being at
> kindergarten helped me to be confident, getting involved in the kids'
> education, like knowing it was OK to ask questions.

Encouraged by Caryll, Kirstie took on the role of committee chairperson and was soon playing an integral part in the life of the kindergarten. Over a 6-year period, Kirstie held a variety of roles at the kindergarten: Committee chairperson, kaimahi, education support worker, and kindergarten chef. During her time at the kindergarten, Kirstie saw her friends Carmella and Makeleta commence studying for their teaching qualifications. The idea that she was capable of tertiary study seemed like an impossibility to Kirstie although she demonstrated a growing interest in her own and other children's learning. However, within a short time, Kirstie was persuaded to apply to do her Bachelor of Teaching degree despite the perceived inconceivability of this prospect for someone from her background and experience. Kirstie commented:

[There were no expectations about education] and I had no
expectations, only one other of my cousins from my whole entire
family has gone off to university—that's it, all the other cousins either
work or have kids so I'm the second person out of our whole family
to actually do tertiary study.

Kirstie is committed to empowering others and sharing her experiences so that others can be inspired. She is encouraged by the changed
reputation of Taitoko Kindergarten and how it is now a preferred
choice for families in Levin—even those from the other side of the rail-
way tracks. Kirstie is thrilled, too, that other parents are being afforded
opportunities similar to her own and taking on responsibilities that
contribute to the sustainability of the kindergarten. For example,
another mother has taken over Kirstie's role as chef, even though her
child is now attending school.

Other families have found opportunities to realise their aspirations
through their involvement with the kindergarten. Carmella, a teen parent who took on the administrative role at the kindergarten, has since
completed a teaching qualification and is employed at the early childhood centre attached to the teen parent unit at the local high school.
Carmella realises the benefits of her experiences at the kindergarten
and that certain practices have become embedded in her way of being.
She took into her employment situations the same philosophy about
building relationships that she encountered at Taitoko. The values and
beliefs she encountered at Taitoko guide her practice as a teacher at a
different early childhood centre. Carmella also recognises she has a role
and responsibility in supporting others:

> We were empowering the community and that's how we all got to
> know one another. We probably wouldn't be here today if it wasn't
> for those sorts of connections and links and recognising that family
> is part of community. It inspires me to do that to others and say,
> 'Hey look you can be a mother and be a teacher and all sorts and be
> whatever you want to be and it's ok and we're here to help you' and
> that's why I think we can be a help because we had the support, it was
> normal, it was natural.

Over the years, families have taken up opportunities at the kindergarten such as kaimahi, coffee-come-play group facilitator, education

support worker for children with disabilities, administrator, and kindergarten chef. They have also been able to pursue other aspirations. To date, five parents have completed their teaching qualification and are now employed in various kindergartens or early childhood centres in Levin. Of the five, four were teen parents who left school without any formal qualifications. A number of other parents have undertaken further study or obtained qualifications and found employment in areas of interest and expertise.

The empowering of these families and their subsequent reach into the wider community has been a significant factor in engendering pride in the community. As Kirstie attested, Taitoko Kindergarten is no longer seen as being a place to avoid. Demographically the community is similar to that of 2005 and statistically the odds are still stacked against families. However, families are being empowered to realise their aspirations through their involvement at the kindergarten. The odds have changed. Mandy neatly summarises the impact of the kindergarten on the community and reinforces the need to replicate the opportunities provided by the kindergarten:

> What the kindergarten has provided in terms of the story that it
> tells, the journey that it's taken, and now what it's achieving—you
> can't measure that in money. And that's to the benefit of everybody.
> Now the rolls are bulging and it plays a really important role in the
> community so we actually need to replicate the kindergarten.

Over the period 2012–14, the Kindergarten Association found opportunities to further influence the provision of early childhood education in Levin. One of the other kindergartens in the area that served a strong Pasifika community was renamed and reconstituted to better reflect the aspirations of the community. The Samoan teacher at Taitoko, and two parents from Taitoko—one Tongan and one Samoan—who had completed teaching qualifications, were all employed at this kindergarten. A community education and care centre that was struggling to remain viable came under the auspices of the Association while a long awaited Teen Parent Unit at a local secondary school opened. The Association won the contract for the early childhood centre attached to this unit. Carmella and Kirstie are both employed at this centre.

What leadership values contributed to the transformation of Taitoko Kindergarten?

In the instance of the transformation of Taitoko Kindergarten, it might be said that 'it got lucky'—lucky that Mandy was able to convince the board to keep it open. However, if we are interested in effective leadership for social justice, we need to look further than a theory of 'luck'. Bourdieu's thinking tool of habitus is helpful in providing some insight into the decision making about and vision for Taitoko Kindergarten.

Habitus, according to Bourdieu (1977), includes the dispositions, rules, and conditioning (social and cultural capital) inherent in family structures and handed down via social transmission. The inclination or propensity to act in a certain way is influenced by the 'structured structures' of the family and groups of our social world. Habitus is how we carry our history within us, how we bring that history into our current circumstance, and how we make decisions to act in certain ways. In short, habitus is the story we live by. Mandy's habitus had been shaped by strong working class values based on collectivity and social justice practices of 'doing good works'. It cannot be denied that in the first instance Mandy's commitment to social justice and her collective and individual habitus structured over time and circumstance ensured that Taitoko Kindergarten was given a second chance. Both of these factors—a habitus steeped in social justice and the altruistic values of an organisation based on improving lives—provided a vehicle for supporting a failing kindergarten and resisting the capitalist ideology that eliminates loss-making components of an organisation.

Caryll's leadership demonstrated dispositions and ways of being that valued the contributions of others and ensured families had opportunities to engage in the life of the kindergarten. These values had come from her upbringing in a small rural community where "everyone looked out for each other" and resources were shared to ensure people's needs were met. The stories recounted by her parents about their early lives gave Caryll an appreciation for the impact of circumstances on successive generations and the fact that not everyone has the same opportunities. Caryll felt her early experiences had a significant bearing on the structuring of her values and beliefs, influencing the "story she lived by."

The strengths-based approach inherent in Caryll's leadership included mentoring of both families and teachers. There is ample research that highlights the benefits of parents being involved in their children's education and that encouraging this involvement during early childhood has long-lasting effects (Belsky, Barnes, & Melhuish, 2007; Bronfenbrenner, 1979; Shonkoff & Phillips, 2000). In many cases, the involvement of families is seen as beneficial, not only for children but also for adults, particularly if there is access to services other than education (Corter & Pelletier, 2010; Press, Sumsion, & Wong, 2010; St Pierre, Layzer, & Barnes, 1995). However, involving families in their children's education can be challenging, especially in communities where families' experiences of education have been negative and in which labels such as 'vulnerable', 'disadvantaged', or 'deprived' stigmatise communities. Caryll's determination that families would feel welcomed and that they would be involved in the life of the kindergarten culminated in family participants replicating opportunities in other contexts. The mentoring that occurred over time for teachers also contributed significantly to Tania's confidence in taking over the leadership of the kindergarten.

Mandy and Caryll both possessed substantial amounts of social capital within the field of early childhood education and, more specifically, the kindergarten. This capital was used to manipulate and strategise in favour of Taitoko Kindergarten and fight the odds so that families could increase their social capital and have the opportunity to be successful in their chosen fields. Bourdieu (1977) ascertained that interactions between individuals in a field were generally about domination and tussles for positions with regard to social, cultural, and economic capital. In contrast, however, individuals with a commitment to social justice are less concerned with 'bettering' their position in a field and more concerned with giving others opportunities by levelling the playing field. There is little evidence in the example of Mandy or Caryll that their primary focus was to enhance their standing or position in the field of early childhood education.

Identifying the characteristics of the habitus of those responsible for decision making at Taitoko Kindergarten has implications for future initiatives aimed at addressing issues to do with vulnerability. Strengths-based approaches to vulnerability view individuals, families, and groups as "people with promise" rather than "people at risk" (Biddulph, Biddulph, & Biddulph, 2003, p. 171). Such an approach assumes individual agency and the use of resources to act on and in the environment to make changes. It interrupts the pathologising of vulnerability (Laursen, 2000) and deflects the tendency to 'blame' individuals for their circumstances. In relation to engaging families in early childhood education and school it is often, as Boag-Munroe and Evangelou (2012) point out, the attitudes or assumptions of the school or early childhood centre, about the family, that results in a lack of engagement rather than the family actually being hard to reach or vulnerable. The authors also suggest that the labelling of families as hard to reach "disguises the complexities of the lives of these families and the factors which led to their disengagement" (Boag-Munroe & Evangelou, 2012, p. 210).

Leadership that is committed to social justice has a high degree of social capital in a field, the ability to recognise an individual's strengths, and the capacity to support and sustain change. These are all key attributes evident in the practices of the leadership associated with Taitoko Kindergarten. These attributes have enabled the utilisation and provision of opportunities that have contributed to an empowered community and opportunities for families to realise personal and professional aspirations.

Questions for readers

- How are families welcomed and empowered?
- How can leadership encourage relationship building with support agencies?
- How can leadership disrupt discourses of vulnerability?

References

Belsky, J., Barnes, J., & Melhuish, E. (Eds.). (2007). *The national evaluation of Sure Start: Does area-based early intervention work?* London, UK: Polity Press.

Biddulph, F., Biddulph, J., & Biddulph, C. (2003). *The complexity of community and family influences on children's achievement in New Zealand: Best evidence synthesis.* Wellington: Ministry of Education. Retrieved from ttp://www.educationcounts.govt.nz/publications/series/2515/5947

Boag-Munroe, G., & Evangelou, M. (2012). From hard to reach to how to reach: A systematic review of the literature on hard-to-reach families. *Research Papers in Education, 27*(2), 209–239. doi.org/10.1080/02671522.20 10.509515

Bourdieu, P. (1977). *Outline of a theory of practice* (R. Nice, Trans.). Cambridge, UK: Cambridge University Press.

Bronfenbrenner, U. (1979). *The ecology of human development. Experiments by nature and design.* Cambridge, MA: Harvard University Press.

Corter, C., & Pelletier, J. (2010). Schools as integrated service hubs for young children and families: Policy implications of the Toronto First Duty. *International Journal of Child Care and Education Policy, 4*(2), 45–54.

Laursen, E. (2000). Strengths-based practice with children in trouble. *Reclaiming Children and Youth, 9*(2), 70–75.

Press, F., Sumsion, J., & Wong, S. (2010) *Integrated early years provision in Australia.* Retrieved from http://www.pscalliance.org.au/Research/assets/ FinalCSUreport.pdf

Shonkoff. J., & Phillips, D. (2000). *From neurons to neighborhoods: The science of early childhood development.* Washington, DC: National Academy Press.

St Pierre, R., Layzer, J., & Barnes, H. (1995). Two-generation programs: Design, cost and short-term effectiveness. *The Future of Children, 5*(3), 76–93.

Chapter 9 Moriah Kindergarten: A turnaround leadership story from survival to success

Debbie Ryder

Introduction

This chapter explores a turn-around leadership story of how an early childhood education (ECE) centre went through a transformation from near closure to success. Through a behind-the-scenes approach to leadership, Heidi Greenwood illustrates a high level of service and sacrifice for the collective good of the development of Moriah Kindergarten. Initially this chapter provides contextual information about Heidi as a leader, and Moriah Kindergarten as a now fully functioning and successful ECE setting. The chapter is also an exploration into the ways Heidi leads for the socially just outcomes with regard to the children and families of the Jewish community that Moriah Kindergarten partly serves. The section on reflections for readers highlights organisational sustainability as a framework by which to understand Heidi's story of turn-around leadership.

Background information

Moriah Kindergarten was established in 1978, and is based in Wellington's Jewish Community Centre. It was only during its first couple of years that Moriah Kindergarten had 100% Jewish attendance. Moriah Kindergarten continues to provide education and care to children and families from the Jewish community, as well as children and families of many different cultural backgrounds. Families come from within the larger Wellington region, and as far as the Kapiti Coast. Moriah Kindergarten operates as a non-profit parent co-operative and caters for a maximum of 25 children aged over 2 years, with four teachers and one parent helper present per day. At the time of this case study, three teachers were registered and ECE qualified, two were registered and Primary qualified (one was currently finishing her ECE qualifications), and one had an international qualification that aligns with the Jewish values-base of Moriah Kindergarten. A management committee of parents governs the centre, with Heidi managing and providing leadership to the committee, parents, teachers, and children. Moriah Kindergarten's mission statement refers to the ways in which the Moriah values (discussed in a later section) guide the actions of the teachers and children as they relate to each other and the world around them. These values are infused throughout the Kindergarten curriculum.

The title Heidi holds as the leader of Moriah Kindergarten is 'Principal'. Originally from Denmark, Heidi now counts New Zealand as her home. She holds a Bachelor of Education (ECE) qualification and is an experienced ECE leader with 16 years' ECE experience in New Zealand and 5 years' overseas. Heidi has worked at Moriah Kindergarten for 16 years, the first 2 years as a teacher and the remaining 14 as leader. Prior to that, she worked in various positions overseas including working at a kibbutz in Israel. Heidi started at Moriah Kindergarten in 2000 as a teacher-in-training, studying through Wellington Teachers, College/Victoria University of Wellington. When the Wellington College of Education sent Heidi to Moriah Kindergarten for practicum experience, it began a rewarding relationship for both parties. When a position came up at Moriah Kindergarten, Heidi was consequently invited to apply. At the same time, she was raising a young family.

In 2010 Heidi was recognised for her strong leadership, by receiving a National Excellence in Leadership Award. This, understandably, was a very proud moment for Heidi, her family, and Moriah Kindergarten, and recognition of the culmination of years of hard work in survival mode.

Leading for socially just outcomes

Throughout the journey from survival to the success of Moriah Kindergarten, Heidi always had the greater needs of the centre at heart. The following sections describe how Heidi put aside self-interest for the greater good of the financial and institutional sustainability of the centre, prioritising reflective practice and professional learning to bring Moriah Kindergarten from near closure to the high-quality special character ECE setting that it is today.

Financial sustainability

Like many ECE centres struggling at that time (2000–02), the enrolment numbers at Moriah Kindergarten began to dwindle. This was also a time of staff changes which, combined with the dwindling numbers, sent warning signals to the management committee that the financial sustainability of the centre was in jeopardy. In a document nominating her for a teaching and leadership award, the Moriah Kindergarten committee acknowledged the leadership and dedication that Heidi displayed during those lean years (at a time when she was not yet a fully qualified teacher):

> For financial reasons, Moriah Kindergarten was on the verge of closure. The other teachers had resigned, but Heidi stayed on, and whilst studying and being a mother to three children, she steered the kindergarten in a new direction with a strong future. [Moriah Kindergarten Committee, 2009]

Heidi (when writing her acceptance speech for the teaching and leadership award—aptly named 'From Survival to Success') also reflected on those same years. She stated:

> It was a dark day in 2002 when I was told that due to dwindling numbers and low finances we had three months to turn Moriah Kindergarten around or face closure. Rising to this challenge was even more daunting, due to the fact that I was newly appointed, relatively inexperienced, a recent immigrant and a full-time student.

Whilst being newly appointed to the centre and still in training, Heidi was also the only permanent member of the teaching staff. During this time, Heidi worked with relievers until permanent staff were employed again. Between the committee and herself, the centre remained open. Heidi reflected on "being a parent cooperative [...] I always appreciated the support and largely voluntary work the parent committee members have contributed over the years." She also commented that, due to financial and team instability, "the early years were very difficult as it became more about survival than high quality." She called this time the "stressful years." However, she also maintained, "due to the special character of our ECE setting, there was always a sense of who we were and what we were there for, and this was a major factor in how we were able to get through those years."

Because of the financial hardship encountered as a result of the dwindling numbers of children regularly attending the centre, sacrifices were made by the teaching staff, the committee, and the Moriah Kindergarten families. There was a shared belief in the importance of children and families spending quality time together; so, although teachers were paid wages during this period, they did not expect any increases and at times would work reduced hours if it suited family needs and the low numbers of children attending particular sessions.

The committee was already giving their time freely to govern the setting and one committee member was doing the cleaning without reimbursement. However, the greatest sacrifice that Moriah Kindergarten had to make lay in its fundamental belief of being open for morning sessions only, so that children could spend time in their home environments in the afternoon. For Moriah Kindergarten a huge decision needed to be made—increase the hours and hopefully stay open—or remain as they were and probably face closure. Heidi commented:

> Moriah Kindergarten is term-based, with a morning session from 8am–1pm. Moriah Kindergarten strongly believed there needs to be ECE centres left in New Zealand that are community based and are not operational all day. Unfortunately, we are finding there are less and less families able to commit to this structure. [Decisions were made therefore to have] an optional afternoon extension until 2.45pm. ECE has become very competitive and our main strength is our special character. We know who we are and have a shared philosophy that is strongly felt throughout the curriculum.

External factors, such as changes to regulatory funding from 100% qualified to 80% qualified staff, were also influencing Moriah

Kindergarten's financial sustainability. It was difficult, therefore, for the centre to practise financial sustainability when they did not know whether they were going to stay afloat in the short term, let alone the medium to long term.

Institutional sustainability

From 2003 onwards, once Heidi was fully qualified, she was able to devote all her time to Moriah Kindergarten and she concentrated on communication within the setting. As parents gained confidence and staff stayed, the centre began to grow again. Heidi began to work with the committee to ensure practices were in place for the institutional sustainability of the organisation. During this time, the centre philosophy remained at the core of Moriah Kindergarten's existence.

With Heidi at the helm ensuring that there was short-term and long-term planning as to how Moriah Kindergarten was going to move out of survival mode, management practices strengthened. Heidi was vigilant in her monitoring and evaluating, ensuring that Moriah Kindergarten's mission statement was being adhered to in all levels of governance, management, and everyday centre practice. From Heidi's award acceptance speech in 2010, we gain further understanding of the critical importance of communication in bringing the centre out of survival mode:

> The first thing we needed to do was to increase our numbers
> and the key to achieving this was to improve and develop our
> communication. How did this happen? I listened ... Active listening
> was applied to current parents, prospective parents, teachers,
> community members and external agencies.

During those early days of transition, Heidi was proactive in her communication. She was quick to follow up on any issues expressed by members of the centre community, in order to alleviate their concerns. Heidi drove the improvement process, with active listening within the newly developing teaching team leading to improved relationships amongst the team and positive relationships with parents. Heidi reassured everyone that they could feel confident to speak up in a trusting environment. For the parents, this meant they were developing "a stronger sense of belonging, an increased understanding of our identity, and a feeling of trust." Heidi reported openly to the community on the progress they were making as an organisation:

We now had quality [practice] and our numbers started increasing as we had renewed energy and enthusiasm in our team and favourable [Education Review Office] evaluations and reports. Parents were now recommending our kindergarten and the word started to spread that we were a quality early childhood centre.

Moriah Kindergarten committee's annual report statement endorses this position: "The kindergarten is now in a very strong financial position … the waiting lists are full and inquiries continue because word is spreading about what a special place Moriah Kindergarten is."

When reflecting on this time of transition, Heidi describes how Moriah Kindergarten moved from barely existing day to day, to having effective systems in place at both the practice and organisational level. It takes committed and determined people to extricate an ECE centre from near closure, and reposition it as a thriving organisation. In Heidi's view, self-review was critical to the teaching team ensuring that Moriah Kindergarten remained a quality ECE setting. However, for Heidi, 'quality' was now not good enough for Moriah Kindergarten; she wanted their practice to be of 'high quality'. Heidi considers that 'high quality' does not just relate to the general practices of running a centre. Rather, she believes that it is in attending to the small details that an ECE setting displays 'high quality'. Heidi talked of the ability for her and her team to anticipate minor issues, and prevent problems occurring:

> It became clear that we were on track and things were going really well at Moriah. However, we were always looking for ways to improve ourselves and Moriah Kindergarten, so we looked at how we could go from quality to high quality. We agreed that it was not just about the big and obvious stuff, it was about the little things. It wasn't good enough to ignore a situation, just because it wasn't urgent. A minor concern got immediately addressed so that it didn't turn into a big one. I started looking out for issues so I could address them immediately. I felt I managed to create an environment where people, teachers and parents felt comfortable and free enough that we could anticipate issues before they even had a chance to arise.

Reflective practice and professional learning

From Heidi's perspective, the essential element of reflective practice was central to supporting the centre to become high performing. For this to occur, teachers met daily for a 1-hour meeting in which they discussed and evaluated their teaching and learning. An outcome of this reflective encounter was the identification of the different strengths of each teacher. Over time, these strengths became areas of leadership for teachers, promoting higher levels of enthusiasm amongst staff and ultimately better outcomes for children and their families. Recruiting daily parent helpers provided an opportunity for parents to be involved in their child's learning at the centre and actively witness the high-quality teaching and learning that occurred. Heidi talks of this as a form of transparency that enabled parents to see their ECE setting in action.

One of the key drivers assisting Heidi to lead Moriah Kindergarten from 'quality' to 'high quality' was a leadership workshop that she attended. When reflecting on what it means to reach high-quality practice and avoid thinking you have learnt everything there is to know, Heidi recalls a quote that encapsulates her approach to professional learning. She likens this to "reaching for the peak of the mountain, but you never quite get there, so … you have to continue to evolve and you have to keep reflecting on what you're doing."

This opportunity for professional development was not early childhood or even education based, but explored leadership generally. Heidi pondered on the issues ECE teachers often encounter when they are not viewed as professionals, and the effect this can have on one's own professionalism and leadership practice. She highlighted the limited amount of leadership training available for ECE teachers. Heidi also expressed her concern that, in some cases, ECE students can come straight out of their Bachelor of Education training and into a leadership role. She considered this to be very problematic.

Once the centre's financial and institutional sustainability was secured, Heidi then focused on Moriah's moral sustainability. Whilst Moriah Kindergarten served children from many different cultures, the centre had the focus of the cultural aspirations of its Jewish community at its core. This focus was uppermost in Heidi's thinking and leadership. The following section illustrates how Heidi's leadership for socially just outcomes for Jewish children and their families led to the ownership of the Moriah values as the soul of the centre.

Moral sustainability

Whilst the overall Jewish values had always been embedded in the Moriah Kindergarten curriculum, it was only after Heidi's professional learning in the leadership area that she realised they needed to 'own' these values. The Moriah Values underpin the mission statement and the philosophy of Moriah Kindergarten. If you were to look on the Moriah Kindergarten website today, you would see that it states: "Our Moriah values guide our actions in the way we relate to others and the world around us, and are infused throughout our whole curriculum."[1] Heidi emphasised that, in the same way that it is important for teaching teams to own their philosophy, it was important for the Moriah Values to be owned by the teaching team; therefore, as a form of professional development, self-review, and team building, the teachers reviewed the overall Jewish values that were already embedded in their curriculum. During this process, each member of the teaching team chose their five most important values and provided a rationale for their choices. The choices were collated and the ones the team all agreed on became the 'Moriah Values'. These were Talmud Torah (Love of Learning), Tikkun Olam (Looking after the World), Chesed (Kindness), Mishpacha (Family/Whānau), Kavod (Respect and Honour), Shmiat HaOzen (Attentiveness), Shmirat HaGuf (Caring for the Body), Hachnasat Orchim (Welcoming Guests), Ma'aseh B'reishit (The Wonder of Life), Ohev et HaBriyot (Loving All Creatures), Bikur Cholim (Helping To Heal), Masoret (Tradition), Lichvod Shabbat (To Honour Shabbat), and V'Samachta B'chagecha (Celebrating Festivals).

Heidi reported that the process the team underwent to gain 'ownership' of these core values drew the team together even more strongly. Once the Moriah Values had been established, it was important to ensure from a strategic perspective that they were embedded in the everyday practice of the centre.

---

1 moriahkindergarten.org.nz/our-values

The role of inquiry in sustaining organisational values

For the Moriah Values to be sustained, it was important that they were embedded in the centre at all levels (financial and institutional as well as moral). It was also important that they were linked to the teaching team's appraisal and teacher registration process. It would be true to say—and Heidi would be the first to admit it—that the documentation involved in the appraisal and registration process is not a strength area of hers. Heidi was a 'talker' and a 'doer', rather than a reflective writer, so, when she attended a Teachers' Council workshop on teacher registration documentation, it would have been with some trepidation. It was just after this workshop that Heidi signed up Moriah Kindergarten to a research project. Teacher inquiry as part of the teacher registration process was very much a 'hot topic' for Heidi at the time, and one she was keen to talk about. Heidi recognised that she would have to find a balance between excessive documentation with which she was uncomfortable, and the need to provide high-quality evidence.

As Heidi began to work her way through understanding 'inquiry,' she weighed up what this might look like for her and her team. Heidi saw the value in inquiry as a process for the whole team to perform, both individually and as a group. Hedges (2007) talks about inquiry as having a community focus which involves commitment and participation. It was clear that Heidi and her team were both community focused and committed. Hedges (2007) also refers to a respect for the viewpoints of all members of the community and the new knowledge constructed through joint inquiry. Inquiry draws on current and prior content knowledge, and working theories are developed and explored through a process of responsive and reciprocal relationships.

As Heidi and their team took ownership and developed their own form of inquiry, they underwent a professional development process similar to that used in developing the Moriah Values. Heidi perceived the inquiry process as a good way for the team to develop together, and as an inclusive process for new teachers joining the team. She saw a place for critical conversations within the inquiry process and, furthermore, discovered a way to simplify the documentation process of inquiry and make this more manageable.

Reflections for readers

This section describes how organisational sustainability links directly to organisational success. Wales (2013) cites Colbert and Kurucz's (2007) conception of organisational sustainability as "keeping the business going", and "future proofing" (Wales, 2013, p. 39). Boudreau and Ramstad (2005) prefer to talk about organisational sustainability as a process of "achieving success today without compromising the needs of the future" (p. 129). From a more practical perspective, Wales (2013) argues that it is important for organisations to develop policies that are aimed at developing a culture of sustainability, by articulating the values and beliefs that underpin the organisation's objectives. Coblentz (2002) describes three key aspects when describing the essence of organisational sustainability: (1) financial sustainability; (2) institutional sustainability; and (3) moral sustainability.

Financial sustainability is seen as occurring when the organisation is aware of: (1) the financial resources it generates; (2) the financial resources it has on hand at any given time; (3) the finances it needs over the short, medium, and long term; and (4) how the organisation will gather any additional funding required. This financial sustainability is viewed by Coblentz (2002) as organisational self-reliance: "a self-reliant organisation … does not compromise its mission" (p. 3).

When referring to institutional sustainability, Coblentz (2002) highlights six essential parts. First, the organisation needs to have a strong mission statement or philosophy that provides a succinct definition of why the organisation exists and what it hopes to achieve. Second, the organisation has a good strategic planning process in place that enables the organisation to "see around the corners" (Coblentz, 2002, p. 2) of the strategic development as related to the mission statement. Third, the organisation has good operational annual plans that are based on the strategic plan. Fourth, these annual plans must enable the production of an annual budget. Fifth, in addition to effective governance, good management is required to organise and direct the efficient use of resources, as related to the organisational mission. Finally, for good institutional sustainability to occur, management needs to be constantly monitoring and evaluating that the mission statement is being adhered to in practice.

With regard to an organisation's moral sustainability, Coblentz (2002) refers to the essence of what makes an organisation work, suggesting: "We can compare institutional sustainability to the body and brain of an organisation. Financial sustainability is the blood that nourishes it. But moral sustainability is its very soul" (p. 4). To achieve moral sustainability the leader requires a clear vision of the mission statement or philosophy, is committed to it, and is able to communicate it effectively to all staff. When the leader exhibits this commitment, the staff will then demonstrate commitment because they perceive their capabilities are being used for the greater good of the organisation. Morale will be high, because staff believe that with unity and strength, all issues can be conquered. It would be evident to anyone entering the organisation that everyone (for example, governance, management, leadership, and staff) behaves ethically, guided by an ethical code of conduct with transparent processes in place for monitoring moral sustainability and managing any issues that arise; with decisions being made based on values that are well known to all (Coblentz, 2002).

Conclusion

As someone who prioritised the collective good of the redevelopment of Moriah Kindergarten above self-interest, Heidi would say that the process of Moriah Kindergarten going from survival to success was not the act of one person alone. Rather, she would say that a number of people were responsible, both collectively and individually. That said, there is one constant element in this story, and that is Heidi. She is a leader with a clear vision of her organisation's mission statement and, through her commitment, was able to communicate that mission effectively to teaching staff, parents, and committee, and the children of Moriah Kindergarten. Because Heidi provided her teaching team with strong moral leadership and openly acknowledged their capabilities, team morale was high. Heidi's attention to the institutional, financial, and cultural identity of Moriah Kindergarten resulted in the embedding of the Moriah Values, which enabled the organisation to progress from bare survival, to keeping the business going, to developing a culture of sustainability. Embedding the social justice values and beliefs underpinning Moriah values means that these fundamental values will not change, even if the leadership of the centre does. This is the sign of ongoing organisational success.

Reflective questions

Reflective questions are offered for consideration as to how Heidi's 'survival to success' story illustrates social justice issues, and Coblentz's (2002) three aspects of organisational sustainability can be viewed from the perspective of your own school or ECE setting:

- How aware are you as the leader of your school or ECE setting's financial sustainability? (For example, the resources your organisation generates, the financial resources it has on hand at any given time, the finances it needs over the short, medium, and long term, and how your organisation will gather any additional funding required.)

- Consider your leadership in terms of the institutional sustainability of your organisation. How does your school or ECE setting's mission statement and philosophy reflect the values and beliefs of all stakeholders? Do you regularly monitor and evaluate the extent to which the mission statement is being adhered to in practice?

- Finally, consider the moral sustainability of your organisation. Are you committed to it and able to communicate your mission statement and philosophy effectively to all staff? Is the mission statement evident throughout all practices that support and develop your teaching team (for example, teacher inquiry, appraisal, teacher registration)?

References

Boudreau, J., & Ramstad, P. (2005). Talentship, talent segmentation, and sustainability: A new HR decision science paradigm for a new strategy definition. *Human Resource Management, 44*(2), 129–136.

Coblentz, J. B. (2002). *Organizational sustainability: The three aspects that matter*. Washington, DC: Academy for Educational Development.

Colbert, B., & Kurucz, E. (2007). Three conceptions of triple bottom line business sustainability and the role for HRM. *Human Resource Planning, 30*, 21–29.

Hedges, H. (2007). *Funds of knowledge in early childhood communities of inquiry*. Unpublished doctoral thesis, Massey University, Palmerston North. Retrieved from http://hdl.handle.net/10179/580

Wales, T. (2013). Organizational sustainability: What is it, and why does it matter? *Review of Enterprise and Management Studies, 1*(1), 38–49.

Chapter 10 Holistic leadership in a high-needs early childhood centre

Ross Notman

Setting the scene

While there is a rightful focus on the leadership of high-needs schools, the obstacles faced by educational leaders in challenging circumstances are no less demanding in early childhood education. This is apparent in the following case study of the Ako Early Childhood Centre, part of the Dunedin Community Childcare Association in New Zealand.

Ako (or Pioneer Lockerbie as it is now known) provides full-day education and care for up to 32 children aged from infants to 5-year-olds. It is located in a diverse socioeconomic area of the city with a predominance of families in the lower income range. It draws on a suburb that has a high rate of unemployed parents whose children live within various family structures, ranging from sole parenting to shared care. The community contains an ethnic mix of people which is predominantly European (68%), Māori (10%), and other ethnicities such as Asian and Pacific Island (21%). While the Ako centre caters for the education needs of its children, families in this area of social and economic disadvantage can access their community hub for support. This hub is operated by the Salvation Army and provides advice and guidance on issues such as budgeting, tenancy, and household insulation. It also provides access to social workers and a public health nurse.

Within this wider neighbourhood group is a key figure who regards herself as "just another member of the community"—Sonya Jephson, Ako's head teacher. She has been in the head teacher position for 10 years after working overseas in Australia and the United Kingdom. Sonya works at least 40 hours per week in her leadership role, not including attendance at external meetings or her own professional learning to keep up to date with developments in the world of early childhood education. She is mindful that she is a mother and needs a work/life balance between her family and her job.

Centre strengths

It is abundantly clear when you watch staff and parent interactions that Ako is a community hub in its own right. There is a high level of parental involvement in the centre's activities, exemplified by large numbers of parents who attend information events, collaboratively building an Ako philosophy of education with the staff, and attending the annual centre Christmas party. A parent identified a strong sense of community for the children and willingness of teachers to use community expertise in meeting children's individual needs.

Unsurprisingly, one of Ako's recognised strengths is its high visibility in the community. It has a strong bicultural focus with opportunities to learn te reo Māori (the Māori language) and an emphasis on identifying and documenting children's strengths and interests, using both features to enhance each individual child's learning and communicating that to parents. Ako's 2015 Education Review Office Evaluation Report states: "The way teachers include children with diverse learning needs is a strength. They show flexibility in the way they work with parents and regularly seek parents' wishes for their children's learning" (Education Review Office, 2015, p. 2). There is a very evident partnership forged with parents in which teachers show particular respect for parents' knowledge of their children.

However, this partnership moves well beyond the common goals of meeting each child's learning needs and the overall educative process. Parents and teachers alike commented on the centre's capability in meeting the social and emotional needs of the parents themselves. This symbiotic relationship between teachers and parents was a particular strength of the centre. It manifested itself in a number of ways. Firstly, the staff put great stock in building trusting relationships with their parent group. They spent considerable time during initial enrolment answering parents' questions and reassuring them about putting their child into early childhood education. Sonya comments on this relationship building:

> For most parents, we do an interview after they've enrolled to see how they felt about the process. Most of them have said it's giving them time because, for some parents, it's a big decision to put their children into early childhood education. So we take our time with our parents. We do a meet sheet, so we get to know the child really well and what's happening for them at home. We encourage photos of the family to come in. We also do amazing social events for our parents, so that could be maybe twice a term, where we share kai [food] together.

This perspective is reiterated in a parent's description of their early days at Ako, and how the centre also met her human need as a mother:

> It made me feel more comfortable. Even though I've worked in the profession, I was quite apprehensive, which felt quite strange because I thought I'm quite confident. But it's different when you have a daughter or a child of your own because it's more emotive and it's harder to separate those things. So I found they were so lovely, they just let me—how would I say it? They just let me … gave me time to relax and just let her be involved in things.

Secondly, the Ako centre goes out of its way to provide easily accessible links for parents to keep in touch with their child's learning. For example, parents can use on-site computers at the centre to access their child's learning progress. For those parents who live at a distance from their family, they have access to their children's learning books via computer links. Thirdly, the centre acts as a social networking hub for parents, both to meet other parents and to converse with other adults in the form of the teaching staff. One of the teachers reflects about parents' situations in an underprivileged community: "If you don't have a lot of money and you don't have a job, then your network's going to be a whole lot smaller. So maybe we're important in that regard."

Finally, the centre acts to support young working parents as they deal with the combined pressures of raising a family and working to provide sufficient income. For some of the first-time parents at Ako, it was their children's teachers teaching them how to raise their children in the form of parenting skills or behaviour management techniques to be used at home.

So how has this early childhood centre been successful in such high-needs circumstances? As is common with leaders in other education sectors, success factors in the Ako centre focus on Sonya's leadership approaches and the strategies she employs with her staff.

Leadership in action

Sonya's predominant leadership approach and associated strategies are built around collaboration, whether that be working co-operatively with her three teachers and education support worker to utilise their respective strengths and experience, or working in tandem with parents on their child's learning capabilities. Her professional relationships with staff are important to her as she positively reinforces good teaching practice or identifies teaching behaviours that require improvement. This she achieves through a steadfast focus on the child. For example: "Tell me about what learning was happening for the children here." She likes to challenge teachers and help them to think about quality teaching practice through learning outcomes.

Alongside this collaborative style of leadership sits a capacity to exhibit strong leadership when required. For example, there are occasions when parents wish to raise concerns face to face with a teacher. In those instances, Sonya asks her staff to redirect the parent to her in her leadership role: "Sometimes you have to put your big boots on and say 'Well, actually no, it's a head teacher's job.'" In this regard, Sonya is very comfortable with the variety of leadership roles she assumes, whether that be as the designated centre leader, mentor, teacher, support person, or learner, in whatever role she is called upon to play. Sonya's leadership philosophy and actions are underpinned by one key aspect: that the people in her community are her first priority. That helps us to understand the implicit nature of this symbiotic relationship that means so much to her:

> You want people to feel valued because, for some of these children
> and their parents, it's their only connection during the day. And so

you want them to feel like they can come in and spend time and feel valued.

There were constant references to a symbiotic relationship that emerges with parents/caregivers as teachers go out of their way to meet the material and emotional needs of parents while supporting the holistic development of their children. This was evidenced by teachers' guidance for parents in accessing social welfare and psychological support for themselves, as well as their families.

Sonya's leadership role in Ako's success

Ako's success factors have been identified through the 2015 Education Review Office report, teacher and parent interviews, and from Sonya's own reflections. The common denominator resides in Sonya's leadership skills that are enacted throughout the centre's daily operation. She is, first of all, an exemplary teacher herself and is firmly focused on providing quality teaching and learning. Commonly identified features include her managerial strengths in being well planned, and understanding and implementing systems processes, such as teacher appraisals and organisational self-review, an ability to have honest and respectful conversations about challenging issues, an open-door policy in which she makes herself available to all, and a willingness to lead by example and to role model good behaviour management practice to younger teachers, such as demonstrating how to intervene effectively in a child's altercation.

Sonya also takes a longer-term view of maintaining quality teaching through a deliberate policy of growing the teachers' pedagogical skills and leadership capacity. She invests resources in staff professional learning both inside and outside the centre. She delegates leadership responsibilities among staff as she is mindful of the need to increase staff confidence across all facets of the centre operation, and of the need to provide for leadership succession planning.

Staff are encouraged to be risk takers in their teaching practice and increase their self-confidence as a result. In this regard, Sonya uses children's risk taking as an example for the staff: "When we're working with children, children are always trying different things. It doesn't matter if you don't succeed. You give it a go and you try out all these theories. That is what we do as teachers. Surely we role model that?"

A second feature of Sonya's leadership contribution to Ako lies in her collaborative leadership skills which have been at the forefront of the collaborative practices firmly entrenched in the centre's organisational culture. A useful example is given in Sonya's description of a forthcoming staff meeting in which a decision is to be made about whether newly purchased toy cars for the children should be left outside or be stored inside:

> So, it's giving everyone the chance to speak and work in collaboration with each other and get a shared understanding of this is what we're going to do with the cars. And I know it sounds quite trivial but they're brand new cars and, for some people, they cost a lot of money and they get buried in the sandpit. Then for some of us it's like, well, actually isn't that how you learn? So we'll have some discussion around that. Eventually we'll come up with a consensus and we'll all be on the same path.

Sonya's ability to build strong interpersonal relationships is another component in her comprehensive set of leadership skills. Knowledge of the local community, its members' family connections, and particular children's circumstances enable her to form a bigger picture of influence that impacts on every child. From a parent's viewpoint, Sonya has a non-hierarchical approach to communicating with parents: "She's really that way, always telling you what's happening, what's going on. I feel like you can talk to her about anything if you need to have a chat."

The quality of relationships between the teaching staff and parents has been a major factor in Ako's success. This positive connectedness with families was exemplified by an interaction with a parent Sonya recalled. A gang member had come to collect their child from the centre for the first time, yet there was no judgement made on the part of the staff of the parent's background. Sonya remarked: "We're not here to judge—that was basically it." This non-judgemental approach to parents was mirrored in teachers' interactions with the children and positive reinforcement of their strengths and interests. Sonya's statement that "actually we don't use the 'fail' word here" was symptomatic of the staff's refusal to engage in any form of deficit thinking about their children's capabilities or social backgrounds "because, as a teacher, you are just working with that child in the moment."

Outside of the centre, Sonya's major leadership role is one of advocacy for the children and families in her high-needs community. She helps locate resources for her centre and community use; she uses social agencies such as Child, Youth and Family and the Salvation Army to maximum effect. She works closely with social workers via the community hub to support families in need, both in terms of pastoral care and in supplying items such as bread, fruit, and vegetables.

Sonya's leadership role in her learning community is pervasive. Importantly, it is underpinned by an educational philosophy in which she wants early childhood education to be about community. A lot of her leadership direction emanates from this simple philosophical underpinning. At a personal level, a driving force behind Sonya's leadership of a high-needs centre is her critical capability to reflect on and problem solve challenging situations, and her self-belief that she can make a difference for children: "I think every day I'm challenged with something different… If I'm challenged in that way and I learn from it, and I reflect and share it with my team, that's got to be great. I definitely think I can make a change."

Her overarching goal is to support and encourage families to meet their aspirations for their child and their family. She wants them to be confident learners and have a sense of social justice when they leave the centre. When asked what she meant by 'social justice', Sonya responded:

> I think they have a sense of what is good for your colleagues, society,
> what benefits everyone really. So that when you're working together,
> that they work in collaboration, they problem solve, they talk
> together, they negotiate and, when they leave, they become citizens
> that want to be part of New Zealand society, really.

Thus, Sonya's leadership role in Ako's success has been broadly influential. Her insistence on a quality teaching and learning experience, her strong collaborative and relational leadership practice, and her community advocacy role all combine to work in the best interests of the children and their families.

Centre challenges

While acknowledging that the neighbourhood demographic is subject to social and economic disadvantage, the Ako centre itself faces internal and external challenges. The internal difficulties revolve around the increasing number of challenging behaviours that children present at the centre. In a recent report, Sonya indicated that 30% have outside agency support to assist them in regulating their behaviours. Some of these behaviours include throwing chairs and tables, children who swear at each other, excessively rough play, and intense tantrums when a child cannot self-regulate. Often, Sonya and her staff work out a behaviour management plan along with the parent so that the child can experience a consistency of reinforcement both at home and at the Ako centre.

Parents in denial about their child's aggressive or antisocial behaviours can also constitute challenges for the teachers. In one case it took Sonya and her teachers 2 years of going back to the parent with actual data about the child's behaviour, "with lots of tears and lots of anger … But we had to keep saying, 'It's not about you as a parent, it's about your child and we want the best for your child.'"

Outside of the centre, a further challenge comes in the form of roll fluctuations from time to time, with implications for the cost of staffing. At the beginning of one year, Ako had lost 10 children within 2 weeks: some children moved out of the area with 2 weeks' notice; three children departed for primary school at age 5; while other children were visiting family in New Zealand for just 2 months. As Sonya comments: "For me as a head teacher, I sometimes find that quite stressful in terms of what happens when your roll drops." Finally, there is the ever-present spectre of reduced central government funding where, for example, centres are left to arrange for non-qualified relievers or have no relievers at all.

Conclusion: Towards the future

Working in an urban area of social and economic disadvantage, Sonya was called upon to exhibit far-reaching leadership skills for children and teachers, and establish positive relationships beyond the educative needs of preschool children. Her leadership success factors have been identified in this New Zealand case study of leadership in a high-needs early childhood setting. However, such factors are complemented by broader considerations which include an absolute refusal to engage in deficit thinking, building symbiotic relationships with parents around social networking and meeting their human needs, and an acute awareness of playing a significant advocacy role for children *and* for the high-needs community in which their families live.

What does the future hold for Sonya and her staff at Ako? Her hope is for the centre to grow and inspire many of the community's children. The reality of continued roll decreases caused by pressures on families, however, places the centre at risk and leads Sonya to contemplate reluctantly the prospect of shifting the centre to another location:

> We may have a physical shift, or we shift our practice, or we try something new, something animated. Or there might be another pool of money somewhere that can give us some other resources. And I guess the preferable future of our centre is that we remain viable really, and that we can sustain what we've got because I think it's pretty special. I think I've probably never worked in an environment like that where it has that whole feel.

Reflections for readers

The current literature acknowledges the increasing complexity of leadership across the school sector and a turnover of teachers in challenging circumstances because the leadership difficulties they face are so acute and relentless (Harris, 2008). The obstacles faced by educational leaders in high-needs circumstances are no less demanding in early childhood education. While we are expanding our knowledge and understanding of educational leadership practice in the school sector, "leadership appears to be a phenomenon that remains an enigma for many in early childhood" (Rodd, 2013, p. 5). As a result, there has been a paucity of research universally, despite a high potential for leadership activity in the early childhood field (Mujis, Aubrey, Harris, & Briggs, 2004). There are calls from writers and researchers in the field for further work on theorising early childhood leadership (Waniganayake, Cheeseman, Fenech, Hadley, & Shepherd, 2012) and in re-conceptualising early childhood leadership in new socially constructed forums (Sims, Forrest, Semann, & Slattery, 2015). This is particularly apposite in the case of leading early childhood centres in communities of complex social and economic disadvantage. Aubrey, Godfrey, and Harris (2013) reflect this leadership complexity when they state: "It is unlikely that one model or a single leadership approach can be appropriate for such a diverse sector; in other words, flexible leadership is the way forward" (p. 26).

While a single case study limits the robustness and generalisability of findings to a wider population of early childhood leaders, it does provide a contextual insight into successful educational leadership in one high-needs setting. So what links can we draw between Sonya Jephson's case study and other research findings in this field?

Firstly, the success factors identified in Sonya's leadership practice are replicated in an Australian research study by Sims et al. (2015) into the understandings of leadership held by 351 Victorian early childhood leaders. Participants were asked to rank important leadership capacities in their sector. The most important capacity for leaders was to act as an advocate for children and families. The ability to develop and sustain relationships was ranked second, while the capacity to develop and manage self ranked third. In addition, Sonya's acute sense of responsibility in her leadership position is paralleled in Thornton's (2011) New Zealand study that explored the collective and collaborative leadership practised at Te Kōpae Piripono, a Māori immersion early childhood education centre situated in New Plymouth. In this setting, te mouri takohanga (being responsible) relates to an individual's attitude and actions: "Being responsible is about being professional, acting ethically and appropriately, being honest, being positive, and being open to others and to different perspectives. This responsibility can be related to the concept of authentic leadership" (Thornton, 2011, p. 107).

These findings link to Notman's (2015) research study of a small sample of New Zealand leaders who identified, from their experience of working in high-needs situations, key skills and dispositions they believed necessary to lead a high-needs school. Principals drew attention to the importance of focusing on the core business of teaching and learning, and on developing positive learning relationships between teachers and students. Common skills referred to among the sample leaders focused on sound planning and organisational practices, strong levels of communication with the parent community in particular, and well-honed negotiation skills in sourcing requisite funding from government social and educational agencies. Above all, there was a consistent call for high-needs leaders to have prior experience of working in a high-needs school environment or to have equivalent life experiences.

Lived experience and experiential learning on the job, especially through taking risks and making mistakes, were seen as prerequisites for successful leadership. The latter factor was essential, leaders believed, in order for a high-needs leader to display their disposition of empathy for, and authentic level of connectedness with, members of their wider school community (Notman, 2015). Allied to this disposition was having the strength of one's own convictions and belief system, not only to sustain themselves in the inevitable pursuit of social justice but also to support their leadership resiliency in the face of demanding and, at times, unrelenting circumstances. One principal noted: "It's not what people think of me that drives me, but rather what I believe in" (Notman, 2015, p. 41).

A second feature in Sonya's leadership skill set was her capacity for critical self-reflection about herself in the job within the Ako community. This relates to Notman's (2011) summary of successful educational leadership in New Zealand which explored factors underlying school principals' ability to sustain leadership success over time through "layered leadership strategies" (Day et al., 2009, p. 200). In this instance, leaders used their reflective time to evaluate their own leadership performance, as well as the staff teaching and student learning. It also appeared that they took time to reflect on aspects of the personal self as well as the professional self, a dimension Gardner (1983) termed 'intrapersonal intelligence': the ability to access and understand one's inner self and idiosyncratic personal emotions, feelings, and aspirations.

A third recurring feature, highlighted in Notman's (2015) exploratory New Zealand case studies of high-needs schools, is the impact of what might be termed *contextually responsive leadership*, the ability to understand and work with socioeconomic and geographic contexts, such as a high-needs environment in rural and urban schools. It reinforces Murphy's (2013) claim that successful school leaders have to deal with a contextual "consequence of plurality—plurality of interests, plurality of values and purposes, plurality of world views" (p. 114). In Sonya's case, there are clear examples of her willingness to advocate for her high-needs children and their families. There is a strong sense of moral purpose within her leadership practice, in which she emphasises the importance of 'community' rather than 'organisation' (Siraj-Blatchford & Hallet, 2014).

Sonya commented that an underlying objective of leading in a high-needs educational context was to guard against the loss of human potential among its children. This prospect is of concern to the New Zealand Ministry of Education, as it applies to other sectors of the education system: "The cost of this loss of human potential is great, as evidenced in the lack of life choices, low self-esteem and limited life satisfaction, disconnection from the community and society … and the ongoing need for social support" (Ministry of Education, 2012, p. 12). In the case of Sonya and the Ako centre, the need to nurture and grow each child's potential is paramount. One can then understand why there is such emphasis on the relationship connection between head teacher, child, parent, and community. The interplay of these spheres of influence is a key ingredient for leadership success in a high-needs early childhood setting.

Reflective questions

Key questions are then put forward for readers' reflection and action:

- How do we best support early childhood head teachers who lead in a high-needs environment?
- How do we guard against the loss of human potential among vulnerable preschool children?

References

Aubrey, C., Godfrey, R., & Harris, A. (2013). How do they manage? An investigation of early childhood leadership. *Educational Management, Administration and Leadership*, *41*(5), 5–29.

Day, C., Sammons, P., Hopkins, D., Harris, A., Leithwood, K., Gu, Q. … & Kington, A. (2009). *The impact of school leadership on pupil outcomes.* Research report DCSF-RR108, UK: Department for Children, Schools and Families.

Education Review Office. (2015). *Evaluation of Ako Early Childhood Centre—09/02/2015.* Retrieved from http://www.ero.govt.nz/review-reports/ako-early-childhood-centre-09-02-2015/

Gardner, H. (1983). *Frames of mind: The theory of multiple intelligences.* New York, NY: Basic Books.

Harris, A. (2008). *Distributed school leadership: Developing tomorrow's leaders.* London, UK: Routledge.

Ministry of Education. (2012). *Shaping education Te Tareinga Matauranga: Directions for education renewal in greater Christchurch.* Wellington: Author.

Muijs, D., Aubrey, C., Harris, A., & Briggs, M. (2004). How do they manage? A review of the research on leadership in early childhood. *Journal of Early Childhood Research, 2*(2), 157–169.

Murphy, D. (2013). *Professional school leadership: Dealing with dilemmas.* Edinburgh, UK: Dunedin Academic Press.

Notman, R. (2011). Building leadership success in a New Zealand education context. In R. Notman (Ed.), *Successful educational leadership in New Zealand: Case studies of schools and an early childhood centre* (pp. 135–154). Wellington: NZCER Press.

Notman, R. (2015). Leadership in New Zealand high-needs schools: An exploratory study from the International School Leadership Development Network project. *Scottish Educational Review, 47*(1), 28–48.

Rodd, J. (2013). *Leadership in early childhood* (4th ed.). Crows Nest, NSW: Allen & Unwin.

Sims, M., Forrest, R., Semann, A., & Slattery, C. (2015). Conceptions of early childhood leadership: Driving new professionalism? *International Journal of Leadership in Education: Theory and Practice, 18*(2), 149–166.

Siraj-Blatchford, I., & Hallet, E. (2014). *Effective and caring leadership in the early years.* London, UK: Sage.

Thornton, K. (2011). Whānau leadership in early childhood. In R. Notman (Ed.), *Successful educational leadership in New Zealand* (pp. 99–109). Wellington: NZCER Press.

Waniganayake, M., Cheeseman, S., Fenech, M., Hadley, F., & Shepherd, W. (2012). *Leadership: Contexts and complexities in early childhood leadership.* Melbourne, Australia: Oxford University Press.

Chapter 11 Leading a school merger in a high-needs setting

Sylvia Robertson

To create a new school is the dream of many an educator. To lead such a development can be viewed with excitement and anticipation. However, in this case, the principal was tasked with leading the unpopular merger of two schools in a high-needs environment.

Falling rolls across a city or region require a rethink about the number of schools needed to service the community. In South Dunedin a major restructure took place that saw the merger of several schools. Mergers are often fraught with controversy. A number of difficult decisions have to be made regarding choice of school to close or retain, retention or redundancy of staff, and appointment of principals. When it was proposed that Macandrew Intermediate merge with Forbury School, tensions ran particularly high. Parents at the contributing primary did not want their children to be part of a full primary. Likewise, parents of the intermediate children had chosen an education they felt best suited the needs of young adolescents. It seemed a no-win situation. Whoever was appointed to lead the new school would surely be up against it.

The school

The result of the merger, Bathgate Park School is a full primary school (Years 1–8) located on the former Macandrew site. It is a decile 3 school located in an urban setting surrounded by a mixture of housing types, parks, and some light industry. The school is newly painted with recently landscaped gardens. A sense of history and tradition is evident with war memorials honouring ex-pupils from the school previously on the site. The front foyer is large and welcoming with an assembly hall adjacent. This multi-purpose space features spectacular artworks reflecting the multicultural nature of the school.

The school opened in 2012 and was designated a school of technology and the arts. The roll has risen steadily since. In 2014, ethnicities represented were NZ European/Pākehā 51%, Māori 34%, Pacific 11%, and Asian 4%. A Māori immersion class opened in 2013 as a result of parental demand. The school's pastoral care and behaviour management programme was developed to reflect the school values of perseverance, respect, integrity, and courage. It is referred to as AROHA. Aroha is a Māori concept that refers to love but also to empathy and compassion (Moorfield, 2011). In the school, aroha is referenced as follows:

Act kindly and gently;

Respect yourself, others, and the environment;

Own your actions. Be honest;

Have a positive attitude;

Always do your best.

The principal

Whetu Cormick is a mid-career principal. He was principal of Macandrew Intermediate before the merger with Forbury School. Whetu has more than 20 years' experience in education, 16 of these years in leadership roles. He was appointed principal in his fourth year of teaching but left this role after 3 years to take up a deputy position in a much larger school. Bathgate Park School is his fourth principalship.

Formative experiences

When talking about his formative experiences, Whetu says he is grateful for teachers who saw potential in him and helped him achieve. His Pākehā father and Māori mother modelled a strong work ethic and emphasised the value of education. He learned from a young age to share, recalling: "I was in a family where you did share. It wasn't all about me." Today Whetu would argue that the school's success was not all about him either. But there is no doubt he has had a hand in it. A number of people and experiences influenced Whetu's leadership style.

At secondary school, Whetu wanted to become a teacher but was advised against this by a guidance counsellor, who told him there were already too many teachers at that time. Instead, he left school to work in the judicial system as a law clerk. After some time overseas, Whetu enrolled at Teachers' College as a mature student, still determined to teach. While at college, Whetu remembers spending 10 weeks with an associate teacher in a new entrant class where he observed that it was possible to have order within chaos. He recalls that this teacher gave him some valuable skills for the work he is doing now. Also influential were university lecturers who gave him specific feedback. The way they encouraged him has helped him be specific in his encouragement of others.

Whetu stresses the importance of respectful relationships and relationships built on sharing and trust. As a young teacher, he was encouraged to apply for a two-teacher principal role. He was successful and eventually, after growing the school to more than double its original size, Whetu moved on to take a position as a deputy in a larger school. This brought new challenges. He recalls building positive relationships with staff as he led the school for three terms while the principal was on leave. Despite his disappointment at not being appointed principal when the position became available, he explains how being the "meat in the sandwich" of a middle leadership position was a worthwhile and pleasurable learning experience. In this role Whetu was able to practise the skills he needed for leadership. It was an apprenticeship that gave him time to develop his ideas about teaching, learning, and leadership.

Values and beliefs

When asked about his philosophy of education, Whetu says it has three parts: students and their learning, what teachers need to do, and community engagement. He believes the community needs to be engaged in the process of developing and guiding the curriculum, and teaching methods. Students need to be at the heart of the learning. He says:

"I'm a great believer that children, children's ideas, children's strengths need to be tapped into. And that they should determine to some degree what learning looks like in the classroom." To this end he is addressing student agency in the school curriculum. For teachers, Whetu believes listening is important. He says that if teachers listen to the community, their students, and colleagues then as they listen they cannot help but start to collaborate with each other. Whether teacher or leader, Whetu concludes it is important to realise that:

> The school is about the kids; it's not about the teachers. I mean we are very important, obviously, but we're not number one. We are just in behind. And so every decision that I make is based on what's best for the child.

When asked whether Whetu feels his values have changed, he says that the values we have from very young become who we are. He says his values are innate. They are part of who he is and "if I was to have to be somebody else then I don't think I could do it. I wouldn't be doing a good job." Here Whetu implies that changing his values would mean becoming a different person. His values direct everything he does, permeate school culture, and reflect AROHA. He reiterates the importance of shared values to ensure everyone is working towards the same purpose.

Whetu speaks of times during his career when his personal values were so challenged he nearly walked away from the job. He had to find a way through these situations and negotiate a comfortable position without feeling compromised. Sometimes this involved taking some time out to get perspective on the situation or talking to a critical friend. In each situation it was renewed focus on what was best for all children in the school, not just individuals or vocal minorities, that helped him find a way through.

Implementing change

Despite other issues challenging schools in New Zealand at this time, such as the introduction of the new National Curriculum (2007) and National Standards (2010), the biggest source of tension for Bathgate Park School was the merger in 2012. The school is still feeling the flow-on effects as the roll continues to grow. Whetu comments:

The school has changed completely from being an intermediate school with a very specific culture and curriculum … to a full primary school where we've had to create a whole new culture and a whole new curriculum to meet the needs of five year olds all the way through to Year 8.

The biggest challenge was bringing two groups of people from two different schools together. This challenge began as he was appointed to the role of principal of the new school.

When it came to making the decision to lead the new school, Whetu felt a sense of vocation, reflecting: "In a way it was a calling because it was meant to be. I was given the job. It wasn't just by chance it happened." He felt the responsibility of the calling immediately. He realised the amount of trust and belief the board of trustees (governing body) had in him and understood the serious nature of the task that lay ahead. Now he is proud of what has been achieved, especially the staff, the work they have done, and their commitment to the students.

Getting there was not always easy. A board member recalls Whetu's determination, saying it took about 18 months to get through the initial phase, and during that time Whetu never assumed things would just happen. She said: "He just put his best foot forward and he got through that." Whetu remembers feelings of sadness associated with the redundancies faced by some of his colleagues. There were feelings of loss around the closure of the intermediate that had been part of the local community for more than 100 years. He felt that there was a need to celebrate the passing of both schools and to acknowledge the value they had contributed to the community over the years. All in all, it felt difficult to celebrate his new position.

Overcoming personal and community concerns

Whetu is honest about the difficulties of leading change. One challenge is staying calm in fraught situations. This skill was developed with time as a result of reflection on past experiences. Now he references these experiences in order to manage emotions, acknowledging that emotional management is not easy and can require a massive effort of self-regulation in some circumstances. On a broader level, facing community resistance in the face of the merger was one such circumstance. Whetu described an emotional public meeting about the merger where he "went into a sort of third person, so kind of like removed myself from it." One board member who witnessed this event recalled that Whetu remained very composed and very positive. Another time Whetu was called out of a meeting to deal with a difficult situation. He described how he had to return to the meeting, sit down and "change his face." He has learned not to carry the drama to the next meeting or the next situation. Instead he tries to switch off, leave "the chaos" behind and move on. Moving on can require considerable courage.

As a young teacher and deputy principal, various principals modelled courage for Whetu. He says these experiences taught him to have the difficult conversations and address issues as soon as they arise. As a young teacher, he observed angry outbursts and learned the importance of being courageous "in a nice, gentle way." He was able to reference some of these early experiences as he dealt with often-fraught situations arising from the school merger. He admits he needed courage to overcome his fears when he started the new school:

> I was scared because it's easy to walk into a school where everything is
> already there and you can just pick up … but actually starting fresh?
> We couldn't just go and recreate what we had because we were an
> intermediate school. And I hadn't been anywhere near primary-aged
> children for 8 years.

He was anxious about his lack of currency with the junior school curriculum but he was also fearful of meeting his new team:

> I was a little bit scared about the first day when all the crew, who are
> in the staff now, about them being here because I didn't know their
> pedigree. They thought they knew my pedigree and so I was a little
> bit scared, if I can use that word, nervous, anxious. But it was just
> fine because we talked and we worked together.

Whetu was apprehensive about the perceptions of the new staff towards their new principal and each other. It was a complex mix of teachers from both campuses and some who were completely new. He recalled how the building work prevented teachers moving into their classrooms immediately. The limited physical space that was available brought everyone together and provided opportunity to talk, plan, and get to know each other. Once the classrooms were completed, everyone worked together as a team to settle each person into their new space.

Another concern was whether the parents would send their children to the new school. Many families had turned their backs on the school in an acrimonious fashion, upset at the merger and choice of new principal. Whetu described how the staff lined up anxiously in the assembly hall on the first day waiting for the children to arrive. Slowly, the children began to trickle in. Since that day the roll has increased to where the Ministry of Education estimated it would settle. Many families have returned to the school despite staying away initially.

Change as a collaborative process

Leading change is difficult. Whetu believes that people need time to understand what change entails and they need the opportunity to contribute to the process. He uses an analogy of growing plants, saying that when people face change you need to "involve them, plant the seed and then help them, or water the plant if you like, to grow it." The key ideas here are involvement and some ownership of what is taking place.

Collaborative relationships are at the heart of change implementation. Whetu stresses the importance of getting on with other people and sharing ideas. He says, "I'm not holding it close," referring to collaboration and distributed leadership practices. Whetu believes that collaboration leads to a sense of ownership, enabling teachers to be more empowered in their teaching. He believes that if everyone in the school community is "interacting, interfacing, talking and listening to one another, then you can only have positive outcomes for the learner." His deputy principal saw Whetu's leadership style change as he increased delegation of responsibilities. She values delegation for encouraging independence and acknowledging strengths but Whetu reflects that the purpose is more about sustainability of culture, programmes, and practices.

At times, more control is needed to ensure implementation of change takes place in a timely fashion. Whetu is keen to involve other people by "letting them be part of a conversation, or developing a project." However, once an idea is developed, he takes control and moves the project into implementation phase. Whetu agrees that perhaps he learned the value of control in his role as law clerk where he directed and led people through courtroom processes. However, he balances control with delegation and collaboration. There is similar balance in his manner, which contrasts formality with friendliness and gentleness. His formality is perhaps also influenced by his early courtroom experiences but it is also about respectful behaviour.

Building relationships

Whetu emphasised the importance of building relationships with the new staff when the schools merged. It was a complex mix of staff from the primary and the intermediate, and some new staff. He said:

> We ended up having about four days of just talking about what our pastoral care and behaviour management values were going to be, and there was lots of debate, and it was really wonderful because we got to know one another.

In this quote he stresses the importance of developing relationships and getting to know each other. He adds: "If I had just thrust documents at them and said, we're doing this, doing that, this is what I've created, it would never have worked because they didn't have buy-in." The idea of buy-in was important during the merger, and is ongoing. Ownership of programmes by staff, parents, and students encourages the sustainability of these initiatives. His deputy principal also acknowledges that by blending internal expertise with external expertise for staff development, Whetu provides opportunities for others to take leadership within the school but also prevents thinking becoming too siloed.

At the core of life at Bathgate is a focus on respectful relationships. Whetu says he does not mind being challenged as long as it is done respectfully. His days in the courtroom were perhaps excellent preparation for the difficult times of the merger where he had to face people behaving in disrespectful, undisciplined ways. He recalls asking staff at the intermediate school to behave with dignity and not to engage with the high emotions that were running. Even though the comments were personal, he recognised it was really the change that was the target. Today he says: "I'm really big on making sure the behaviour is respectful and dignified." He says he will challenge behaviour that is not and he expects others to do this too.

Leadership qualities

Visibility

Whetu is a highly visible leader. He is aware of being in the public eye and having a visible presence in his school. Whetu talks of teaching as a performance: "You're on a stage. People are watching you but you've got to be yourself. You can't make out you are somebody else … you have to be who you are." When asked if he feels he has a number of different identities, Whetu replies that there probably are different faces but he emphasises, tapping his heart, "Whetu is here." He says he is not putting a completely different face on at every forum, but he will change behaviour depending on the situation and audience. This variety of audiences includes students, colleagues in the local area, staff, and board. Although there is a different dynamic in each of the situations, he says: "I'm the same person everywhere [but in] the conversations that we have from one forum to the next, the tone is going to be different."

Visibility enables Whetu to see and be seen but he is also an active listener. He says that when challenged he tries hard not to get defensive but to listen. These challenges come in many forms. In staff meetings, if an issue arises, such as playground behaviour, he writes it down and addresses it later at assembly. The public follow up is important. It is clear to everyone that the person has been listened to and the issue addressed. For Whetu, careful listening, note taking to support memory, and taking action that confirms the listening, are a trio of skills he has developed over the years. It was not always this way. He recalls early in his career: "I had it already sewn up, what was going to happen. And I probably just would have launched in, and then got defensive, argumentative with people." This leadership behaviour changed over time in response to context.

Consistency is important for those with a visible presence in leadership. Whetu notes that "because you are dealing with people all the time, different people, there has to be some sort of consistency in the way you behave." This was particularly challenging at the time of the merger when Whetu drew deeply on his beliefs, values, and strategies for emotional management in order to maintain that consistency. He reflects on the difficulty of maintaining consistency:

I guess you've got to kind of put on a bit of a performance [even] if you're not feeling your best. You've still got to breathe and be calm and listen all the time; even if that person is quite frustrating, or you're tired, hungry or whatever.

Again, he emphasises the need to manage himself emotionally and to be able to move from one situation to another without carrying any emotional upset or concern into the new situation. This was not always easy and required the use of deliberate strategies such as setting pace and priorities, maintaining high standards of professionalism, using reflective practice, being open and transparent, and thinking strategically.

Setting pace and priorities

Whetu talks about the importance of being internally and externally organised at all times. He has learned to measure his responses and, although frustrated by interruptions requiring urgent attention, he has learned to prioritise. He says: "Whether it be people, or paper, or children, everyone's got to take their place." Learning to prioritise enables him to remain fully focused on the issue at hand. He now moderates his response in terms of expectations of his staff. But the change has been a two-way process in that as he became more accommodating, his leadership team became more confident to express their concerns. His deputy principal notes that change happened for both Whetu and his team. She says the change process influenced Whetu: "He realised that things have to work at a particular pace. He's very aware of staff dynamics, staff capability, and knowing when to put the accelerator down and when to put the brakes on." In recognising this, she sees that Whetu is attuned to the paradoxes of leadership. He is able to recognise that sometimes the pace of change will be fast and at other times it can happen slowly. Sometimes it is appropriate to collaborate, whereas, at other times, direction is needed.

Professionalism

For Whetu, professionalism is following the agreed-to values or norms of the school. However, it goes beyond the school gate, in that professionalism is evident in how the staff present themselves as educators to the community. He believes that dressing appropriately for the task is one way of showing respect for yourself and also for those you represent:

I know that young people are looking at every move that we make and if we're not presenting ourselves professionally, they notice it. They notice when we are not looking our best and they notice when we are not behaving our best.

Professionalism is about being honest and genuine. To model this, Whetu says: "We challenge behaviour or we challenge situations, which we know are not right as per our values. And we do it in a respectful way." He gave examples such as expecting that everyone (including himself) would pick up litter in the playground or challenge an inappropriate remark. Whetu admits appearances or performances can be deceptive and he can be easily charmed. He seeks support when recruiting and uses his listening skills to moderate and seek glimpses beneath the surface of the candidate to establish an all-important match in values.

Reflective practice

Whetu is highly self-aware. Although he says he does not care that people might be observing, judging, and thinking, the perceptions of others have been influential over time. He comments on the value of feedback:

> The negative feedback is probably more important than the positive feedback because we're just being patted on the back and reassured. We already know that aspect there but it's the stuff that we're not so good at that we really need to work on.

Despite this view Whetu values encouragement and positive feedback. An adviser who was helping at the school told him that, despite the challenges presented by the merger, the teachers were remarkably calm, the classrooms orderly, and the school was humming. He also shared comments made by some junior school children when asked to describe their principal. They said: "He is kind, gentle, he shakes hands at assembly, he wears suits, he's got a little bit of no hair." Although he laughed at the time, these special comments obviously meant a great deal.

Personally, Whetu tries to focus on improving perceived areas of weakness such as managing emotional response. However, he acknowledges it can be hard to change. He says of the appraisal process that "the same feedback keeps coming through." In this instance, Whetu is talking about communication skills, yet others described him as the consummate communicator. His deputy principal thinks appraisal has been beneficial. In the past it was sometimes difficult to get Whetu to consider their ideas but now he listens and responds. Again, this is an example of a leadership behaviour that has changed in response to context.

Whetu looks for positive outcomes. He uses reflection to put a positive spin on difficult times. For example, any disputes with his board are treated positively. Whetu says that such disagreements only serve to strengthen the board and his relationship with them. Disagreements provide opportunity to reflect "on our policies and our practices at school and how we react to situations in future." Reflection provides the opportunity to learn from experience and to enhance resilience.

Open and transparent leadership

Knowing each other is important. Whetu stresses it is important that others understand what drives his high expectations:

> I'm myself. Yes. What you see, this is who I am. People know
> about me, who I am and [pause] personally. They know who I am
> professionally. They know what to expect. They know what I think
> about teaching and learning.

In this statement, Whetu stresses the importance of being frank and honest. People can understand his expectations because they know him. By being explicit about his values and modelling these in all situations, then children, staff, and parents have a clear understanding of his expectations. Whetu values honesty in others. He encourages staff to talk to him if they have a concern about something. He encourages openness and transparency and "dealing with it" rather than letting situations simmer.

Strategic thinking

In terms of vision, Whetu talks about the need to consolidate what has been achieved before starting a review process that will enable the school to grow for the next 5–10 years. He says it is important to see the big picture for implementation of new initiatives but it is also important the school is sustainable. He wants the next principal to have "some guiding documents and a culture they can feel when they enter, when they take over." Whetu's capacity for big-picture thinking means he can create readiness in his staff for change. His deputy principal says that his careful planning means they achieve the goals set. This was affirmed by a board member who referred to Whetu's capacity for strategic planning, saying: "He's very much a planner so everything's done in advance, planned in advance." In this way, change becomes a continuous process. There are few surprises or unexpected changes in the school.

Towards the future

Since the merger, the Education Review Office (ERO) has provided a report about the school. The report is positive and details success in a number of areas:

> The principal and staff have worked hard to develop a positive school culture, pride in the new school and high expectations for behaviour. The school's guiding motto is AROHA and this is constantly talked about. This and the school values are very evident in the respectful way adults and children relate to each other. (Education Review Office, 2014, p. 3)

Also noted is the way the school embraces the diverse cultural background of its pupils. Significantly, "Māori students in this school achieve better than other groups of students in the school in reading, writing and mathematics" (Education Review Office, 2014, p. 7). The report continues to describe how the adults and students in the school value Māori language and culture: "In a short time adults in the school have built a culture of manaakitanga (caring) and whanaungatanga (family-like relationships)" (Education Review Office, 2014, p. 7). The adults (and children) who built this culture have been instrumental in making the school the success it is today. Leadership of the school has been fundamental in this process.

Whetu adapted his leadership style in response to change. He is better able to moderate the way he responds, work collaboratively, and he can clearly articulate personal values and beliefs. His beliefs about education are unchanged. He says: "I always believed that parents and community should be involved in how we shape the learning programme and how we shape the school to support the learner." Still important to him is getting on with other people, sharing ideas, knowledge, skills, and understandings with others. Whetu continues to be passionate about his work. His emphasis is on building sensitive, respectful, and positive relationships in which the first priority is the children. He recognises that development of a new school culture is gradual. It involves high levels of trust, respect, and collaboration between all stakeholders. The experiences and leadership qualities that Whetu brought to this challenging appointment have influenced the way the school has emerged, fully fledged and successful.

Reflections for readers

This case study illustrates a dilemma in leadership between constancy and change. On the one hand, constancy in purpose and beliefs is signalled as a factor in successful leadership. For example, Notman and Henry (2011) found successful principals are "comfortable in articulating their values and professional philosophies in public" (p. 379). This level of comfort indicates a well-established set of values that are easily recognised by everyone in the school community. For Whetu and his staff, developing a set of values around the concept of aroha provided clear guidelines for practice in the school. AROHA instilled a sense of constancy that continues to underpin every decision made in the school. On the other hand, leaders face pressure to adapt to meet the demands of practice. Leaders must be "flexible rather than dogmatic in their thinking within a system of core values" (Leithwood, Harris, & Hopkins, 2008, p. 36). Flexible leaders can adapt the way they think, act, and feel in order to meet the changes and challenges inherent in their role. Flexibility can support resilience. Day (2014) contends that values and beliefs are fundamental to leadership. He argues "resilience allied with moral purpose" (p. 653) is key to sustainable leadership in high-needs situations. Yet to align moral purpose with resilience can be problematic. To be resilient may mean adapting personal and professional identity "to better persevere through future encounters with hardship" (Christman & McClellan, 2012, p. 650). Tension may arise when demands for flexibility challenge personal values and beliefs. Leaders may struggle to resolve dilemmas that arise between constancy and change.

In this case study, Whetu found his values were challenged as he led the merger of two schools. He had to adapt actions, modify feelings, and reframe thinking in order to meet the demands of practice. However, his beliefs and values remained constant. Instead, other aspects of his leadership approach were adapted to better respond to the challenges of the situation. In making these changes, Whetu demonstrated flexibility, resilient behaviour, and the skills of a learner as he developed strategies to persevere in his role. Among these strategies, reflective practice allowed him to gain perspective and reframe situations more positively in order to move forward. Barnett and O'Mahony (2006) describe this practice as a "combination of hindsight, insight, and foresight" (p. 501). Critical reflection enables the leader to learn from experience, gain new knowledge and understandings, and be prepared for future hardship. Thus Whetu was able to continue to guide and support his community through the merger despite the personal challenges he faced. Throughout it all, he maintained moral purpose, determined to do what was best for the students of the school.

Whetu developed a culture that would benefit not only the students but also the staff and local community. His first priority was building positive relationships. The Kiwi Leadership for Principals model (Ministry of Education, 2008) reminds us that relationships are central to leadership. The four qualities of leadership—pono (self-belief), ako (learning), awhinatanga (guiding and supporting), and manaakitanga (leading with moral purpose)—are reflected in a school's culture, pedagogy, systems, and the partnerships and networks developed to support learning. However, these aspects of school leadership are reliant on the capacity of the leader to adapt to change, and face challenges with determination and resilience. When leading a school in a high-needs situation, the tension that arises between constancy and change may be accentuated, thus heightening the complexity of the role for those charged with implementing change. Personal leadership practices and beliefs may be thrown into sharp relief as change is implemented. Very often the leader feels pressure to adapt practice and beliefs. Those who lead change may find themselves changed by the process. The challenge of the merger has honed Whetu's leadership skills and practice, but he has stayed true to his values. His values align with the school values of AROHA. For school communities facing challenge and change, Whetu emphasises the importance of "being respectful and kind and gentle to one another, and always doing your best and being honest."

Reflective questions

Reflecting on your practice in terms of constancy and change, you might like to consider the following questions:

- Can you clearly articulate a moral purpose for your school or centre?

- What would you consider important values to guide the development of a new school?

- Can you recall a leadership experience where you felt a dilemma between a desire for constancy in beliefs and values and the need to change?

- In what circumstances have you used strategies to manage emotionally challenging situations?

- How has leading change changed you and your leadership practice?

References

Barnett, B. G., & O'Mahony, G. R. (2006). Developing a culture of reflection: Implications for school improvement. *Reflective Practice, 7*(4), 499–523. doi:10.1080/14623940600987130

Christman, D. E., & McClellan, R. L. (2012). Discovering middle space: Distinctions of sex and gender in resilient leadership. *Journal of Higher Education, 83*(5), 648–670. doi:10.1353/jhe.2012.0035

Day, C. (2014). Resilient principals in challenging schools: The courage and costs of conviction. *Teachers & Teaching: Theory and Practice, 20*(5), 638–654. doi:10.1080/13540602.2014.937959

Education Review Office. (2014). *Bathgate Park School education review.* Wellington: Author. Retrieved from http://www.ero.govt.nz/review-reports/bathgate-park-school-30-04-2014

Leithwood, K., Harris, A., & Hopkins, D. (2008). Seven strong claims about successful school leadership. *School Leadership and Management, 28*(1), 27–42. doi:10.1080/13632430701800060

Ministry of Education. (2008). *Kiwi leadership for principals: Principals as educational leaders.* Wellington: Author.

Moorfield, J. C. (Ed.). (2011). *Te Aka: Māori-English, English-Māori dictionary* (3rd ed.). Auckland: Longman/Pearson.

Notman, R., & Henry, A. (2011). Building and sustaining successful school leadership in New Zealand. *Leadership and Policy in Schools, 10*, 375–394. doi:10.1080/15700763.2011.610555

Chapter 12 Transcending the personal and political: Provocations

Michele Morrison, Ross Notman, and Rachel McNae

Each case study in this book stands alone. The leaders portrayed in these narratives, and the authors who collaborated with them in the re-storying of their lived experience, bring unique worldviews and particular theoretical lenses to bear. It is appropriate that readers should do the same. In this concluding chapter we seek not to prescribe meaning nor constrain interpretation but to highlight three emerging themes: complexity, agency, and action. Rather than summarise each case we select examples that evoke and illustrate the points we wish to make. We consider the implications of complexity, agency, and action for practitioners, policy makers, and the education profession (pre- and in-service). Finally, we conclude with a series of provocations that we hope will ignite passionate debate, professional commitment, and the political will necessary to reach national consensus over what we mean by social justice and how we best go about achieving this.

Complexity

Byrnes' (1998) definition of complexity as "the domain between linearly determined order and indeterminate chaos" (p. 1) will bring more than a wry smile to leaders charged with meeting the needs of those least well served by the education system and turning around less than optimal performance indicators. The leaders in this book are well acquainted with complexity and a tendency for the spaces between to resemble more closely the edge of chaos than a semblance of order. Complexity arises because "outcomes are determined not by single causes but by multiple causes … [which] may, and usually do, interact in a non-additive fashion" (Byrne, 1998, p. 20). This necessitates a move away from reductionist approaches to change, towards holism and acknowledgement that the whole is often greater than the sum of its constituent parts.

Complexity is inherent in the different education sectors in which leaders work, and in the individual settings located within these sectors. Spanning early childhood, primary, intermediate, and secondary sectors, the settings represented in this book include not-for-profit and for-profit kindergartens and early childhood centres, low- and high-decile schools, and faith-based and secular organisations that are variously thriving, striving, and sometimes barely surviving. Two of the three early childhood settings, for example, are situated in areas of social disadvantage, and two faced insolvency and imminent closure. The assumption that the two settings possess these features in common is an erroneous one, however.

Immersed in distinctively local settings, leaders face many opportunities and challenges that are context-specific. That is, they arise from the particular attributes of, and circumstances facing, the school or organisation. These include factors that are primarily endogenous to the school or organisation such as student roll composition, staffing profile, material resources, organisational history, and culture; and those that are exogenous in origin such as national education policy, accountability regimes, and geographic, demographic, and economic variables. Leaders themselves constitute an integral dimension of context. Their personal and professional biographies shape leadership habitus, espoused commitment to discourses of equity and justice, and the ability to enact these in their daily work. Taken as a whole, then, context describes the idiosyncratic mix of external environmental conditions, internal organisation dynamics, and leaders' prior experiences/backgrounds that together constitute fluid, relational leadership environments (Morrison, 2017).

Leaders bear ultimate responsibility for discerning context, determining which contextual factors are of pressing as opposed to peripheral concern, and responding accordingly. The merger of the local intermediate and primary schools into a full primary school (Years 1–8) made forging a new organisational identity Whetu Cormick's immediate priority. Sheralyn Cook inherited a school under statutory management with fractured relationships and significant debt, while organisational stability lent support to Penny Deane's focus on democratic pedagogy and the authentic application of 'real-life' learning in cross-cultural communities of difference. For Lisa Morresey, the annual turnover of half her intermediate school roll intensified an urgent need to address anti-social student behaviour and create safe learning contexts.

The cases in this book also demonstrate the competing priorities that add complexity to change processes. For Heidi Greenwood, one of the greatest tensions lay in endeavouring to remain financially viable whilst holding fast to values underpinning opening hours. Steve Berezowski grappled with the potential for individual and collective conceptions of social justice to inflict injustice. Reconciling these dilemmas requires leaders to live with ambiguity and juggle multiple rights.

The nature of home-centre/school relationships adds another dimension to complexity. In some settings, relationships are such that the education provider becomes a central locus of community, whilst in others it lies on the periphery at best and is estranged at worst. Healthy home-centre/school partnerships thus require leaders to reach out and communities to reach in. Sonya Jephson and Caryll Resink saw the potential for their early childhood settings to meet the multiple needs of children and their parents, providing the latter not only with a point of connection but also opportunities to develop personally and professionally.

In Wairoa, iwi agitation for the school to join Te Kotahitanga met sympathetic reception in a principal willing to countenance a positive counter-narrative, to be guided by the community, and to engage in authentic power sharing. This example serves to illustrate the conscientisation and resistance arising from multiple educational realities and adds yet another layer to complexity. Honouring Treaty obligations involves more than surface manifestations of bi-culturalism in curriculum and organisational rituals; it requires culturally responsive leadership and pedagogies that enhance distributive, cultural, and associational justice.

Agency

The impetus for change among these social justice and high-needs cases has multiple points of origin. One motivating factor for change came in the form of previous lived experience on the part of the school principal. For Robyn Curry, it was a strong background in special needs work that drove her leadership directions. In the case of Steve Berezowski, it was a number of key experiences in his personal biography that shaped his later commitment to social justice practice (for example, his working class origins; early friendships with Māori families; and a particular work ethic directed towards helping families with financial disadvantage).

An overarching impetus for all case study leaders lay in their sense of moral purpose, a concept summarised by Bezzina and Tuana (2014) as "the commitment to ends that express underlying values and ethics" (p. 283). A clear moral vision was a key factor behind Heidi Greenwood's success in re-vitalising her early childhood centre. Her underlying concern for children with special needs was a driving force in doing what was right in the interests of her students. It was this shared vision that sustained centre staff in challenging times as they worked reduced hours with zero wage increases. Similarly, Penny Deane's "immense moral fortitude" and deep-level understanding of her students enabled her to lead from that place. Sonya Jephson, too, had strong moral convictions about how she would lead her early childhood centre in a holistic and multifaceted way (for example, her refusal to engage in any form of deficit thinking about her disadvantaged children; her willingness to meet the human needs of parents; and her preparedness to take up a significant advocacy role for children and their families). This call to advocacy in the face of perceived social injustice takes a moral position by speaking on behalf of those people whose voices are not always heard. This public action is outlined by London (2008), whereby:

> Advocates speak out and take action to effect change, often overcoming resistance. They increase awareness of an issue and generate positive attitudes. They recruit and retain volunteers who become advocates themselves. They influence government policies.

They deliver services, raise money, and build organizations to sustain their advocacy goals. (p. 314)

This advocacy role is driven by an inherent passion that "seeks to change people's values and beliefs from self-centred to other-centred" (Theoharis, 2008, p. 16). It is also underpinned by the fusion of leaders' personal and professional values where there is often little that separates the person of the principal from their leadership practice. Allied to these belief systems of leadership in social justice settings is the concept of leading from a position of hope. Sheralyn Cook sees positives in this leadership perspective for her students: "You have the opportunity to do whatever you want to do, and be whatever you want." This stance links well to the field of positive psychology where agency or motivation is the belief about one's personal capacity to reach desired goals (Leithwood & Mascall, 2008). Nowhere has this been better illustrated in New Zealand than in Christchurch school leaders' resilience and sense of hope following the trauma of the 2010 and 2011 earthquakes (Notman, 2015).

Action: Leadership strategies for success

Successful strategies employed by school and early childhood leaders centred around three thematic areas: parental involvement, leadership professional practice, and personal dispositions.

One of the central findings about leading for social justice in high-needs educational environments was the consistently high priority given by leaders to encouraging and sustaining parental involvement in their child's education. This finding is reflected in Robinson, Hohepa, and Lloyd's (2009) seminal work that advocates for the influential role played by parents and whānau in helping to improve students' learning outcomes. As an example, Sonya Jephson is one such leader who maintains a high level of parental involvement in her early childhood centre. She accomplishes this by means of information events, access to children's learning books via the internet, and a community-wide Christmas party to celebrate the year's end. In what could be described as a symbiotic relationship with her parents and community, Sonya enhances this relationship by addressing parents' social and emotional needs; offering daily access to each child's learning; and sharing her suggestions for parenting skills or behaviour management techniques to be used at home. In similar fashion, Wairoa College leaders engaged with their Māori elders, establishing whānau-like relationships with their community, while Steve Berezowski fosters student cultural identity by links with the local marae and by using community elders as a teaching resource.

The area of leadership professional practice reveals key strategies employed by leaders and teachers who work in challenging environments. Collaborative work practices with their staff, together with the process of distributed leadership, is a common approach. Heidi Greenwood made full use of shared curriculum leadership responsibilities, while Robyn Curry re-established roles for her senior leadership team based on individual strengths in curriculum and in special-needs/student behaviour. Knowing how and when to adapt the pace of change was another leadership strategy, ably demonstrated by Whetu Cormick in his merged school. His staff commented: "He's very aware of staff dynamics and staff capability, and knowing when to put the accelerator down and when to put the brakes on."

Another uniformly shared strategy was that of leadership reflective practice. This was typified in Lisa Morresey's case study in which she blended reflective practice and emotionally intelligent leadership, "where the leader is readily able to recognise their own and other people's emotions in order to use this awareness to guide their leadership thinking and behaviour." In a number of cases, the concept of emotional intelligence (Goleman, Boyatzis, & McKee, 2002) is a major part in the success of these New Zealand leaders. They have an ability to 'read' people in a social justice and high-needs context, and understand the impact of working alongside them instead of forcing an accommodation to suit their preferred leadership approach.

The use of longer term strategic thinking was an effective strategy used by Sheralyn Cook at her Waikato school. Here, she used strategic goal setting and a shared vision with staff to support school-wide decision making. Other effective leadership strategies across the 10 cases included having honest and respectful conversations about difficult issues; building a supportive school/centre culture; and growing teachers' pedagogical skills and leadership capacity. This latter strategy was exemplified at Wairoa College where school leaders prioritised tikanga Māori and resourced full-time te reo teachers. In addition, Penny Deane and Steve Berezowski took the theme of social justice directly to their students by developing opportunities for them to safely explore and question issues of injustice in their own school context.

The case studies revealed personal dispositions that were associated with leading for social justice. These personal characteristics included being passionate about teaching and learning; treating adults and children with respect; exhibiting an authentic ethic of care that resulted in students' experience of school as a safe and secure place. They also demonstrated leadership courage, as in Sheralyn Cook's case, where she was required to "make decisions that, for some, might seem unfair, but it was the right thing for them at a particular time." Finally, there was a fundamental belief among all the school and early childhood leaders that students could improve their learning capabilities. As Robyn Curry asserted: "I so believe in these kids—they have so much potential." And it appears a unifying objective for leading a high-needs school or centre in a socially just environment that case study leaders fought vehemently to guard against the loss of human potential among their students.

Future thinking, implications, and provocations

Leading in, through, and for social justice

One of the aims of this book was to share the stories of educational leaders who lead for social justice across and within a variety of contexts. In doing so, it was our hope that some enduring ideals and understandings might be synthesised. While this has been the case, what has also emerged is recognition of the complexities shaping each educational leader's response and commitment to leadership for social justice. The rich accounts of leading for social justice and working in high-needs settings, along with the diverse strategies of engagement shared in this book, contribute to an evolving tapestry of understandings. Given the contextual and highly personal nature of each leader's response, what learning can we draw from these cases for those tasked with the responsibility of leading in educational settings? With an eye to the future, what are the implications for educational leaders and how might you, as a reader of these cases, draw inspiration, hope, and a sense of activism to lead for social justice yourself?

Recognising the complexity of social justice leadership

Just as the introductory chapter illustrated broad and varied definitions of social justice, it has become clear that simply defining and
illustrating socially just leadership is not enough for sustained socially
just leadership. The experiences of these leaders illustrate the complex moments in which they found themselves; where responses and
actions were demanded in often extremely challenging circumstances,
and deep-seated values and moral stances were continually challenged.
Working from a socio-ecological perspective (Ministry of Education,
1999), educational leaders can explore, notice, and become attuned to
the complex interrelationships and interdependence that exists between
themselves, others, and society.

It has become apparent across each of these cases that the intersec-
tionality of experiences (Crenshaw, 1989), which continue to sustain
and support a form of resilience founded on a sense of moral purpose,
are frequently bound by often-static structures that fail in their respon-
siveness and relational attributes to address aspects of injustice. Day
(2014) argues that:

> diverse and sometimes competing demands of policy, local context
> and educational values not only challenge the breadth of qualities,
> knowledge and skills possessed by leaders, but also test their
> adaptivity, flexibility and intellectual, and emotional energy on an
> everyday basis. (p. 638)

The educational leaders in this book have illustrated that leading
for social justice in high-needs contexts transcends traditional leadership perspectives, as they deliberately work to shift power and address
inequality at multiple levels. Consequently, implications arise for those
involved in education in its broadest sense, whether at the 'chalk-face',
in the playground, around the boardroom table, or preparing teachers and leaders for challenging environments. When examining these
implications, the contextual nuances cannot be ignored.

Implications for leaders

Leading for social justice happens within and across relationships.
Re-establishing, reforming, and sometimes rupturing relationships
can be central to the work of a socially just leader. Understanding and
sometimes brokering existing and historical relationships from within

the context can provide insight into some of the enabling or limiting factors that continue to perpetuate unfairness and inequality. Knowing and working within and across these relationships can play a key role in forming and implementing initiatives (for example, exploring ways to gain community support for raising student achievement).

Leading for social justice requires time. Often this element is in opposition to the pressured, fast-paced decision making that schools and centres demand of leaders. In the 'busyness of the business', time presents itself as a precious commodity in educational contexts. In order to sustain leading with socially just intent over time, it becomes essential to carve out space for personal and professional reflection and decision making. Taking time to search for information and explore options in decision-making processes, along with embarking on consultation, is important as sometimes the most obvious pathway ahead is not the most appropriate. In a job that demands so much, ensuring a commitment to personal wellbeing is important. This means surfacing, reflecting upon, and making sense of the affective, emotional, personal, and physical demands of the work, as well as seeking an alignment between personal values, moral purpose, and actions (McNae, 2017).

Implications for policy development

Encouraging educational leaders, teachers, students, families, researchers, and policy makers to participate in a national conversation about socially just leadership would elicit and illuminate multiple perspectives. This can help to craft a national definition of social justice in education, which can be aligned to a more inclusive achievement agenda informed by research and lived experiences. The development of policy that connects schools to their communities, promotes inter-agency support, and reflects upon challenging structures that perpetuate inequality (for example, the perceived stigma attached to the school decile rating system), can create shifts in discourses about the shape of success and achievement. Conversely, acknowledging what is already working within school and communities is essential, together with supporting the continued resourcing of educational initiatives known to work.

Implications for researchers

Researchers play a key role in exploring the complex intricacies of social justice in education. In examining global discourses and specific contextual elements, researchers can propose research agendas that attend to areas that have been overlooked, marginalised, or excluded from current educational debates. Using a lens of social justice to refocus educational and political agendas on the core business of education, researchers have an obligation to explore unjust practices and interrogate the current landscape of socially just educational leadership. By conducting research with approaches that align with social justice elements (for example, narrative inquiry, voice, ethnography, and case study) researchers can shift from a focus on skills and traits to exploring and embracing the human side of leadership.

Implications for pre-service education providers

Pre-service teachers are an accessible point of contact and an influential unit for change. Working with pre-service teachers to surface morals and values is a critical step in the formation of teacher identity. If teachers are given the opportunity to explore the concept of social justice, learn the skills needed to interrogate contexts and stereotypes, and develop strategies for enhancing resilience, while building a sense of activism, this group of future educators will likely become more attuned to injustice. It is this group of teachers who will plan and lead activist interventions when they encounter injustice.

Recent rapid expansion in early childhood education provision has seen newly qualified teachers taking up leadership roles without adequate experience or preparation. This suggests that the inclusion of leadership and management learning in pre-service programmes is necessary, not just for organisational sustainability but for personal wellbeing and socially just outcomes as well.

Implications for leadership preparation

The importance of uncovering personal values, life narratives, and moral underpinnings cannot be emphasised enough. In order to build leadership understanding and develop new knowledge about leading for social justice, recognising, understanding, and validating justice in its more diverse forms is essential. Once identified, issues of injustice can be more readily addressed. As such, preparing leaders for the holistic nature of their job becomes paramount. This includes developing the abilities to attend to the social, cognitive, and behavioural needs of young children, along with the parenting needs of adults, creating new awareness of what it means to be a learner in a particular context. Supporting aspiring leaders to become attuned to issues of social justice and injustice in its multiple guises is an essential part of their leadership formation.

Provocations

To conclude this chapter, we share a number of provocations that reflect the complex and frequently under-theorised aspects of the work performed by educational leaders in the name of social justice. Based on the high-needs and social justice contexts shared in this book, the following reflective provocations are offered.

Reflecting on freedoms and opportunities for educational leaders

The work of the educational leaders in this book encourages us to reflect upon the opportunities and freedoms teachers and leaders have to create contexts, cultures, and curricula that pay attention to and address issues of social justice. It becomes clear that social justice leaders are deliberate and intentional in supporting and enhancing the wellbeing of others. This being the case:

- How might educational leaders examine their own contexts from the inside?

- What role might a critical friend play in drawing attention to everyday happenings and disrupting patterns of thinking and behaviour?

- What opportunities do educational leaders have to reflect upon their emotive responses to leadership? How do leaders maintain emotional resilience in the face of challenging situations?

- How might leadership in educational settings create space for affective responses as well as policy responses?

- In what ways are principals supported in their work as they lead a school from a crisis situation to one that is flourishing?

- What actions do leaders of high-needs workplaces take in order to advocate for families, as well as take care of children's educational needs?

- What is the interplay between personal values and actions when responding to policy initiatives aimed at particular changes, that may exclude and marginalise further students?

- How do educational leaders manage the tensions between policy-driven decisions and their own personal values?

Reflecting on possibilities and responsibilities

Embarking on leadership for socially just outcomes is demanding. However, as contributions in this book have indicated, it is extremely rewarding and, of course, necessary. This work and its associated value can take various shapes and forms. Most importantly, whatever the action(s), the work must place children/students and their wellbeing at the centre. Teachers have a critical role to play in this regard:

- How might teachers design, integrate, and implement curricula from a position of social justice, so that learning experiences are more enduring, authentic, and meaningful?

- In what ways do teachers model leading for social justice in the classroom and what is the impact of this?

- Who is responsible for initiating conversations about social justice within the school and beyond the school?

- What role can students play in addressing the tension/disjuncture between curriculum demands, testing outcomes, and real-life experiences?

- To what extent are teachers accountable for raising levels of student performance? How can other participants assist in a child's learning (for example, parents and government agencies)?

Reflecting on context and cultures

Developing an awareness of socio-cultural and historical discourses requires courage and resilience. Having a firm understanding of contextual influences—the things that constrain or support leadership for social justice—can support educational leaders in their decision making and reflective practices:

- How do you respond to the contention that the less powerful and less privileged best understand how to transform oppressive relationships?

- What does it mean to be a Treaty partner in education?

- How do we ensure that success today does not compromise success in the future?

• Conversely, how do we ensure that benefit for future student cohorts does not come at the expense of current students?

Future research possibilities

Providing opportunities for individual teachers and leaders to develop and enhance their understandings about social justice is critical. Beginning and drawing attention to a national conversation about social justice, while simultaneously generating dialogue within local contexts, could support this learning. Further research exploring what this conversation might look like at a national level would be useful. Who would be involved in this conversation? Whose voices get heard in the cacophonic calls for support, aid, and attention; and perhaps more importantly, where are the silences? What is not being said?

Interestingly, few of the case study participants in this book recognised their educational leadership preparation programmes as sources of learning or support in their work for social justice. Investigation into the ways educational leaders are prepared for their roles, along with an in-depth exploration of the content, access to, and evaluations of educational leadership programmes, should be seen as valuable.

The core business of most social justice work revolves around students. There is a need to examine social justice work/leadership from the *perspective of students*. What does this work mean for them? What might they learn through their involvement? Future research might include uncovering student perspectives of social justice from within their school settings and exploring notions of activism and agency through the actions of the students themselves.

There is also a need for educational leaders to become attuned to and better understand the key intersecting characteristics of *injustice* that impact on young people, staff, and the wider community. Research that examines these characteristics could provide valuable insight into broader contextual debates about social justice leadership.

Further research into global discourses about social justice, combined with greater attention to a diverse array of cultural contexts, could open up further conversations about social justice which are more culturally responsive and culturally located. Those working in educational leadership may then be better positioned to understand how broader physical, social, political, economic, ethical, and cultural contexts enable and constrain their efforts to enhance social justice and meet high needs in schools and centres.

Considering how and when this research might take place becomes central to this research agenda. Already, a sense of urgency permeates communities where injustice surfaces. Noticing and responding to this urgency become critical elements of an educational leader's and a researcher's way of working. However, efforts to illuminate and investigate issues of social justice in high-needs settings must be socially just in themselves, seeking to create change where possible, in ways that recognise context, are sensitive to individual needs and, above all, are initiated and enacted for the right reasons. Research methodologies that value and embody spaces for the personal narratives of leaders also support multiple realities and allow the complexities of this work to be examined deeply and carefully.

Concluding remarks

The cases shared in this book create a starting point for what we anticipate will be many new conversations about leading for social justice in high-needs contexts. It is our hope that insights into the lived experiences of these leaders provide an opportunity for readers to reflect upon their own contexts and valuable leadership endeavours. It may be that these insights support the validation of experiences infrequently talked about and assist leaders to surface silences and disrupt systems and discourses that continue to perpetuate injustice in the workplace.

Traversing the delicate balance of diversity and unity, community and individual needs, along with conceptions of personal and political action, the complexities associated with such work are less obvious. The responsibility for educational leaders to remain attuned, reflective, and engaged in local, national, and international conversations about leading for social justice is crucial to meeting current and future challenges. This book comes with the hope of triggering a call for action that focuses our attention on the humanity within leadership, and what it means to lead in socially just ways, for socially just outcomes for every student.

References

Bezzina, M., & Tuana, N. (2014). An insight into the nature of ethical motivation. In C. M. Branson & S. J. Gross (Eds.), *Handbook of ethical educational leadership* (pp. 282–293). New York, NY: Routledge.

Byrne, D. (1998). *Complexity theory and the social sciences: An introduction.* London, UK: Routledge.

Crenshaw, K. (1989). Demarginalizing the intersection of race and sex: A black feminist critique of antidiscrimination doctrine, feminist theory and antiracist politics. *University of Chicago Legal Forum, 1*(8), 139–167.

Day, C. (2014). Resilient principals in challenging schools: The courage and costs of conviction. *Teachers and Teaching—Theory and Practice, 20*(5), 638–654.

Goleman, D., Boyatzis, R., & McKee, A. (2002). *The new leaders: Transforming the art of leadership into the science of results.* New York, NY: Time Warner.

Leithwood, K., & Mascall, B. (2008). Collective leadership effects on student achievement. *Education Administration Quarterly, 44,* 529–561.

London, M. (2008). Leadership and advocacy: Dual roles for corporate social responsibility and social entrepreneurship. *Organizational Dynamics, 37*(4), 313–326.

McNae, R. (2017). School leaders making sense of the 'self' with[in] social justice: Embodied influences from lived experiences. In P. Angelle (Ed.), *A global perspective of social justice leadership for school principals* (pp. 251–270). Charlotte, NC: Information Age Publishing.

Ministry of Education. (1999). *Health and physical education in the New Zealand curriculum.* Wellington: Learning Media.

Morrison, M. (2017). Conceiving context: The origins and development of the conceptual framework. In P. Angelle (Ed.), *A global perspective of social justice leadership for school principals* (pp. 43–64). Charlotte, NC: Information Age Publishing.

Notman, R. (2015). Seismic leadership, hope and resiliency: Stories of two Christchurch schools post-earthquake. *Leadership and Policy in Schools, 14*(4), 437–459.

Robinson, V., Hohepa, M., & Lloyd, C. (2009). *School leadership and student outcomes: Identifying what works and why. Best evidence synthesis iteration.* Wellington: Ministry of Education.

Theoharis, G. (2008). Woven in deeply: Identity and leadership of urban justice principals. *Education and Urban Society, 41*(1), 3–25.

Suggested further reading

In addition to the references listed at the end of each chapter, readers will find the following of interest:

Bogotch, I., & Shields, C. M. (Eds.). (2013). *International handbook of educational leadership and social (in)justice*. Dordrecht, The Netherlands: Springer.

Bolman, L. G., & Deal, T. E. (2013). *Reframing organizations: Artistry, choice and leadership* (5th ed). San Francisco, CA: Jossey-Bass.

Boston, J., & Chapple, S. (2014). *Child poverty in New Zealand*. Wellington: Bridget Williams Books.

Clarkin-Phillips, J. (2011). Distributed leadership: Growing strong communities of practice in early childhood centres. *Journal of Educational Leadership, Policy and Practice, 26*(2), 14–25.

Cranston, J. (2013). School leaders leading: Professional responsibility not accountability as the key focus. *Educational Management Administration & Leadership, 41*(2), 129–142.

Crippen, C. (2010). Serve, teach and lead: It's all about relationships. *Insight: A Journal of Scholarly Teaching, 5*, 27–36.

Fasoli, L., Scrivens, C., & Woodrow, C. (2007). Challenges for leadership in Aotearoa/New Zealand and Australian early childhood contexts. In L. Keesing-Styles & H. Hedges (Eds.), *Theorising early childhood practice: Emerging dialogues* (pp. 231–253). Castle Hill, NSW: Pademelon Press.

Fraser, D., & Deane, P. (2010). Making a difference: Agents of change through curriculum integration. *set: Research Information for Teachers, 3*, 10–14.

Lumby, J., & Coleman, M. (2016). *Leading for equality: Making schools fairer*. London, UK: Sage.

Ritchie, J. (2016). Qualities for early childhood care and education in an age of increasing superdiversity and decreasing biodiversity. *Contemporary Issues in early childhood*, 1–14. doi: 10.1177/1463949115627905

Thornton, K. (2010). School leadership and student outcomes: The best evidence synthesis iteration: Relevance for early childhood education and implications for leadership practice. *Journal of Educational Leadership, Policy and Practice, 25*(1), 30–40.

Thornton, K., Wansbrough, D., Clarkin-Phillips, J., Aitken, H., & Tamiti, A. (2009). *Conceptualising leadership in early childhood education in Aotearoa New Zealand*. Wellington: New Zealand Teachers' Council.

Zimmerman, J. (2011). Principals preparing for change: The importance of reflection and professional learning. *American Secondary Education, 39*(2), 107–114.

Editor and contributor biographies

Editors

Rachel McNae, PhD, is an Associate Professor of Educational Leadership and Director of Te Puna Rangahau o te Whiringa—The Centre for Educational Leadership Research at the University of Waikato. Rachel's research agenda is founded on and shaped by a firm belief in social justice. Through her teaching and research Rachel seeks out and interrogates the relational aspects of leadership, championing leadership encounters that are authentic, culturally responsive, and meaningful. Rachel has developed, taught, and co-ordinated a range of postgraduate and higher degrees in education and leadership, receiving numerous awards for her research and contributions to the field of educational leadership, including the New Zealand Educational Administration and Leadership Society Presidents Research Award, the European Foundation Award for Management and Development Outstanding Research in Leadership and Strategy, the New Zealand Educational Leadership Meritorious Service Award, and, most recently, the New Zealand Educational Administration and Leadership Society Visiting Scholar.

Michele Morrison is a Senior Lecturer in Educational Leadership at the University of Waikato. Informed by extensive practitioner experience, Michele's research and teaching focus on the professional formation of educational leaders through dialogic praxis. Michele prioritises educative processes that privilege lived experience and a concern for the humanity of leadership. This has led her to develop and teach postgraduate coaching and mentoring qualifications, to research tertiary pedagogies for leadership formation, and to explore the centrality of context in change leadership, leadership for social justice, and educational governance. Michele is currently editor of the *Journal of Educational Policy and Practice*. Recently published work features in *Working (with/out) the system: Educational leadership, micropolitics and social justice* (Information Age Publishing), *Mentoring in early childhood: A compilation of thinking, pedagogy and practice* (NZCER Press), *Democratic ethical educational leadership: Reclaiming school reform* (Routledge), and *A global perspective of social justice leadership for school principals* (Information Age Publishing).

Ross Notman is Professor in Education and Director of the Centre for Educational Leadership and Administration at the University of Otago. He has worked extensively in principal appraisal and in principal support groups through activities such as coaching and group support networks. His major research interests focus on teacher and school principal development, particularly in the field of the personal dimensions of principalship. Ross is the New Zealand director for the International Successful School Principalship project and the International School Leadership Development Network project. He is a member of the editorial board for the *Journal of Educational Leadership, Policy and Practice* and *Leadership and Policy in Schools* (USA). Ross presents at international leadership conferences and has edited significant publications about successful leaders in New Zealand schools.

Contributors

Zac Anderson is a Master of Education candidate and staff member with the University of Waikato. Her Master's research focuses on the role of first time secondary principals in achieving educational reform in Aotearoa to enable Māori students to pursue their potential as Māori. Zac has been a teacher, middle leader, and deputy principal prior to working as a kaitoro (facilitator) with Kia Eke Panuku. As tauiwi (more recent immigrant), Zac embraces her obligations under the Treaty of Waitangi to engage in building educationally powerful connections with Māori students and their communities.

Mere Berryman MEd, PhD, ONZM is an Associate Professor at the University of Waikato. Her early research involved collaborative work with schools, Māori students, their families, and communities through the formation of culturally responsive relationships. This work merged with the inception of Te Kotahitanga, and was further built upon in 2014 with Kia Eke Panuku. This iterative professional development initiative aimed to promote Māori students' educational success as Māori by combining understandings from kaupapa Māori and critical theories with policy. Ongoing evidence of educational disparities for Māori continues to make this work a priority. Mere publishes extensively in this field.

Christopher Branson holds the Professorial Chair for Educational Leadership in the Faculty of Education and Arts and is Director of Catholic Leadership Studies in the La Salle Academy at the Australian Catholic University. His research interests include those of the nature and practice of leadership, ethical leadership, educational leadership, personal and organisational values, leadership for social justice, and organisational change. Along with many chapters and journal articles, his published books include *Leadership for an age of wisdom* (Springer), *Leading educational change wisely* (Sense Publishers), *Handbook of ethical educational leadership* (Taylor & Francis), and *Leadership in higher education from a transrelational perspective* (Bloomsbury, in press).

Jeanette Clarkin-Phillips has been involved in early childhood education for many years as a kindergarten teacher and lecturer. Her Master's research case studied a professional development programme based on a distributed leadership model, while her doctoral thesis explored the potential of early childhood centres to support adult aspirations. Jeanette is currently directing a research project exploring the concept of distributed leadership with kindergarten and education and care centre teachers. She has co-directed, with Professor Margaret Carr, three Teaching and Learning Research Initiatives (TLRIs), and is a member of the research team recently awarded a Marsden fund to investigate children visiting museums.

Sheralyn Cook is an experienced primary school teacher and educational leader. Most recently, Sheralyn has held the role of principal of a rural primary school in the Waikato region. In 2015 she was awarded the NZEALS President's Research Award and for her doctoral research is currently researching principals' experiences of leading high-needs schools in New Zealand, specifically the effect and impact these interventions have had on them professionally and personally. Sheralyn is based at the Centre for Educational Leadership Research at the University of Waikato while on a TeachNZ Primary Principal Study Award.

Deborah Fraser is a recently retired Professor of Education at the University of Waikato who has dedicated her academic career to investigating aspects of inclusive education, curriculum integration, creativity, spirituality, and the arts in education. As the recipient of numerous prestigious awards (Sir Peter Blake Trust Leadership, Fulbright Scholar, and the New Zealand Council for Educational Research/UNESCO Beeby Fellowship), Deborah's contribution to the field of education is longstanding and her impact enduring. She is the co-editor of New Zealand's leading text in teacher education, *The Professional Practice of Teaching* (Cengage), spanning 20 years and five editions, and has been the principal investigator of seven externally funded research projects.

Lisa Morresey is Principal of Mount Maunganui Intermediate School. She has over 20 years' experience teaching in primary and intermediate schools, both mainstream and immersion, and taught for 2 years in a high-needs, inner city East London school. Lisa has served as an Assess to Learn (AToL) and health/physical education adviser. A first-time principal in 2010, she now mentors beginning principal colleagues. Experience as an Air Training Corps flight sergeant and rugby player has heightened Lisa's awareness of equity and inclusion issues. She credits her family with enabling her to be the best principal she can be.

Sylvia Robertson is a highly experienced primary practitioner with research interests in teacher education and school leadership. She has held teaching and leadership roles in New Zealand, Australia, and the United Kingdom, in both state and independent school systems. Sylvia recently completed doctoral studies at the University of Otago where her research investigated principal perceptions of self and change. She has recent and forthcoming publications in pedagogical leadership practices, and the transformation of professional identity in experienced primary school principals.

Debbie Ryder is a Senior Lecturer at Te Rito Maioha Early Childhood New Zealand where she teaches in the Postgraduate Diploma in Leadership (ECE). Debbie has also lectured across a range of courses and programmes in her 11 years' experience in the tertiary education sector. She previously taught for over 20 years in ECE settings, predominantly managing and leading two community-based early childhood centres. Currently, Debbie is undertaking a collaborative research project with colleagues, *Leaders Growing Leaders*, and she is in the final year of completing her PhD.

Cathy Wylie's main research focus has been on policy and its impacts for school leadership, teaching, and students, and the longitudinal study Competent Learners, which has provided important understanding about different trajectories of engagement and achievement in learning. Her 2012 book, *Vital connections* (NZCER Press), makes a cogent case for system change to strengthen all our schools and counter uneven educational opportunities. She is a Chief Researcher at the New Zealand Council for Educational Research.

www.ingramcontent.com/pod-product-compliance
Lightning Source LLC
Chambersburg PA
CBHW080043280326
41935CB00014B/1774